ISRAEL AND THE DIASPORA
IN JEWISH LAW

Essays and Responsa

STUDIES IN PROGRESSIVE HALAKHAH, VOLUME VI

Also in this Series

Walter Jacob and Moshe Zemer (eds.) DYNAMIC JEWISH LAW, Progressive Halakhah - Essence and Application

Walter Jacob and Moshe Zemer (eds.) RABBINIC - LAY RELATIONS IN JEWISH LAW

Walter Jacob and Moshe Zemer (eds.) CONVERSION TO JUDAISM IN JEWISH LAW - Essays and Responsa

Walter Jacob and Moshe Zemer (eds.) DEATH AND EUTHANASIA IN JEWISH LAW - Essays and Responsa

Walter Jacob and Moshe Zemer (eds.) THE FETUS AND FERTILITY IN JEWISH LAW - Essays and Responsa

//
950.04
jac

ISRAEL AND THE DIASPORA IN JEWISH LAW

Essays and Responsa

Edited by

Walter Jacob and Moshe Zemer

Freehof Institute of Progressive Halakhah
Pittsburgh and Tel Aviv
Rodef Shalom Press
1997

Published by the Rodef Shalom Press
4905 Fifth Avenue
Pittsburgh, PA 15213
U.S.A.

Copyright © 1997, Solomon B. Freehof Institute of Progressive Halakhah

4905 Fifth Avenue
Pittsburgh, PA 15213
U.S.A.

4 Rehov Levitan
69204 Tel Aviv
Israel

Library of Congress Catalog Card Number 96-071375

Jacob, Walter 1930-

Zemer, Moshe 1932-

ISBN 0-929699-09-2

Dedicated

to

Burton E. and Geraldyn R. Belzer
of Torrance, California

and

to the memory of

Leon Finley ז״ל

TABLE OF CONTENTS

PREFACE v

INTRODUCTION vii

ISRAEL AND THE DIASPORA 1
    Leonard Kravitz
THE LAND, THE LAW, AND THE LIBERAL CONSCIENCE .. 19
    John D. Rayner
"THEY SHALL NOT MOUNT THE WALL FROM EXILE" ... 47
    Aviezer Ravitsky
ALIYAH AND *YERIDAH* IN RABBINIC SOURCES 93
    Judith Hauptmann
ALIYAH: CONFLICT AND AMBIVALENCE 113
    Moshe Zemer
THE PRIMACY OF THE DIASPORA 149
    Walter Jacob

SELECTED REFORM RESPONSA

1. Israeli Flag on a Synagogue Pulpit 167
2. An Old Israeli Flag 171
3. Hebrew or English at an Israeli Service 173
4. Popular Israeli Song in the Synagogue 175
5. Jerusalem Soil into the Grave 177
6. Visiting Israel 179
7. *Aliyah* in the Face of Parental Opposition 185
8. Questions from Israel on Proselytism 189

CONTRIBUTORS 197

PREFACE

We continue to be grateful to the Rodef Shalom Congregation for supporting the Freehof Institute of Progressive *Halakhah* and its assistance in technical matters connected with the publication of this volume. Our special thanks to Nancy Berkowitz who has carefully copy edited and proof read this volume. We wish to thank Barbara Bailey for her efforts with the typescript for this volume as well as previous volumes.

INTRODUCTION

Judaism's ties to a specific land make it unique among world religions. From the days of Abraham, Judaism has been associated with the Land. It was not even Abraham's native land, but one he entered at God's command. The Land of Israel, which belonged to the people of Israel, was mentioned often in the Bible. Yet most Jews throughout our long history have lived outside the Land, in the Diaspora. This circumstance has raised the tensions that are the subject of this book.

Other religions have ties to holy sites that are places of pilgrimage, but only a few adherents ever chose to settle in them permanently. Christians established a monastery on Mount Sinai and in other locations associated with the Bible or the life of Jesus, but only a handful of monks reside at Sinai. The same is true for the followers of Islam who pilgrimage to shrines associated with Mohammed, but make no effort to settle there.

For us as Jews, God's promise to the patriarchs combined the blessing of the people with the gift of the Land. That promise was reiterated again and again, and the "Promised Land" became the goal of the entire people as it wandered through the desert from Egypt. Our annual cycle of Torah readings has reinforced the promise; it is the dominant and underlying theme.

It was therefore natural for modern Zionism, a nationalist movement akin to many others, to awaken an interest in the Land of Israel. It was very different, however, because it was not a nationalist movement against the "overlord" and oppressor, but one that sought settlement in a distant country almost totally unknown except through biblical imagery. Zionism added the thought that we could be "like all other people" with a land we would call our own and in which we could do as we pleased.

except through biblical imagery. Zionism added the thought that we could be "like all other people" with a land we would call our own and in which we could do as we pleased.

Our century, with the Holocaust and various oppressions, brought a critical need for a permanent place of Jewish refuge, and the State of Israel has fulfilled that role. This has gained the support of Jews throughout the world. Many oppressed Jews have settled in Israel, but others have rejected it for a new Diaspora existence.

Our association with the Land of Israel, however, has always been balanced by the idea of a people "chosen" for a broader mission in the world. The aspect of particularism that associated Jews and Judaism with the Land is countered by a universalism that seeks a role in the broader world and that represents an equally majestic dream. The Diaspora has been seen in this light—also as part of the Divine plan, which uses us and our life for a broader purpose.

The prophets of Israel initially saw expulsion from the Land as Divine punishment but later understood it as part of God's plan, and therefore normative. God would resettle the people of Israel in our own land in the Messianic Age, but until this Divine intervention occurred we should live out our destiny scattered throughout the world.

Through the ages, economic forces and human inertia kept us in the lands where we had settled. This response began in the days of Ezra and Nehemiah (400 B.C.E.). They received permission for Jews to return to Israel and to rebuild the land as well as the Temple, but the vast majority decided to remain in Persia. In that early period the Temple continued to attract Jews to make pilgrimages in the land; but later, when the Temple had been destroyed,

Jews found they could live a complete Jewish life anywhere, even while praying for the restoration of the Temple in the Messianic Age. Jews in small numbers continued on pilgrimages to Israel, but few moved to the Land.

We therefore possess two competing visions of where Jewish life should be lived: the Diaspora and the Land of Israel. Each could be fully justified. Until modern times and the reestablishment of the State of Israel, these thoughts were more theoretical than actual.

Reform Judaism has emphasized the universal aspect within Judaism. We began as a religious movement two generations before Zionism; we sought equality in the lands where we lived at the same time as we wished to influence those lands. We felt that our mission in the world could be best accomplished through living in the lands where we found ourselves; we would move the world toward our Messianic dream. That optimism was best expressed by the American Reform movement at the beginning of the twentieth century.

Reform and Zionism therefore clashed. By the 1930's the universal and particular tensions of Judaism were felt more strongly within the Reform movement, and the particular and the universal came into balance. The Columbus Platform of 1937 gave a place to Zionism within Reform, but without the demand that we personally resettle in the Land of Israel. Zionism has grown stronger within Reform ranks through ARZA, through the placement of the headquarters of the World Union in Jerusalem, and through the establishment of Progressive congregations and several Reform kibbutzim in Israel. All Reform rabbis train in Israel for a year, and a separate group is educated to serve the Reform movement there. Yet the vast majority of Reform Jews, along with our Orthodox and

Conservative counterparts, continue to live outside the Land of Israel with no regrets and with no intention of moving.

We must therefore constantly deal with the realities of our Diaspora existence and the ancient Messianic dream of the Land of Israel, for some restated in modern secular Zionist form. This tension has been an important theme in the *halakhic* literature; this book will deal with it.

ISRAEL AND THE DIASPORA: SACRED AND PROFANE

Leonard Kravitz

To speak of Israel and the Diaspora: sacred and profane, is to anticipate that Israel and the sacred will be paired as will be the Diaspora and the profane. Reflection, however, will temper that anticipation; we shall see that the pairing of terms is problematical: historical and conceptual problems are intertwined. We know too much; we ask certain questions that arise from the outlook we have as modern Jews. Our sense of history has shown us that terms, whether describing people or places, as Israel and the Diaspora, or presenting evaluations, as "sacred" or "profane," arise in contexts that set their meanings. As the contexts change, the meanings are affected. We wonder as we deal with these terms if we are to deal with them in their original contexts or if we are to deal with them as the developing Jewish tradition dealt with them in various contexts. There are further problems of meaning: if we contrast "Israel" and the "Diaspora," we suggest that the words refer to geographical areas. What of the people who lived in those areas? Were they "sacred" or "profane"? If we use such terms, can we ask if they carry the same aura as the terms *kadosh* and *tamey?* What makes something sacred? If something was considered sacred in the past, would we consider it sacred in the present? Conversely, if something was considered profane in the past, would we consider it profane in the present?

Were we to say that the Land of Israel is sacred, what would be the basis of such a judgment? Would it be our sense of being part of an *am segulah,* a particular people? Would it be our involvement with the literature of that people? Would it be our faith in the One, Who, according to that literature, promised that land to that people? Would we assert that the Land itself is somehow special, different, and therefore conducive to unique experiences that we, for want of a better word, will call ""sacred?" If the Land is sacred, does it follow that that which is outside the Land is therefore "profane?" To whom, when, and where does such a term apply? What disabilities, if any, are connected with it? Can one with equanimity dwell in a profane place? What happens if Jewish communities, for whatever reason, find themselves ensconced for long periods in various geographical areas outside the Land? Does that affect their sense of sacred and profane when applied either to the Land of Israel or to the Diaspora?

We know that Jewish literature is of different kinds, emerging from different places at different times. Such differences reflect the vagaries of Jewish history and the fate of the Jewish people. Jewish creativity was found inside and outside the Land. The Bible and the Mishnah were written inside the Land; the Gemara that became authoritative, the *Bavli,* was composed outside the Land. Many aggadic *midrashim* were composed in the Land; all medieval Jewish philosophy was composed outside the Land. Many of the responsa and most of the codes were composed outside the Land; the code that was composed in the Land, the *Shulchan Aruch,* did not become authoritative until it received its commentary, *Mappah,* which was composed outside the Land. If the tag of "profane" were applied to the Diaspora, it could not be applied to that which was produced in the Diaspora.

Thus, Jewish history renders problematic the categories of sacred and profane. The Diaspora, however profane, did produce the sacred, but so did the Land, even when the Children of Israel were in the Diaspora. From the Land the sacred was maintained as a memory through the literature created in the Land—the Bible (particularly the Torah), the Mishnah, and the *Midrashim*—and also through that literature that had originated in the Land and that has often been undervalued, the liturgy. The *Siddur* was available to all, learned and unlearned, and was read and recited three times a day. Through the liturgy, the Jewish people could do what the Psalmist could not: sing a song to Zion and a song to the Lord,[1] even in *admat nechar*—even in the Diaspora.

Another issue complicates the discussion the Land of Israel as sacred and the world outside as profane. It is the existence of the State of Israel as it is, a modern state existing in the here and now. Whatever we may think of Israel, it is filled with *people,* not illustrations in some holy book. Its people are like people everywhere, saints and sinners, religious and secular, good and bad. It is difficult to apply the term "sacred" to such a variegated group. There are aspects of Israeli life to which the term "profane" might easily apply. Shall we say that the beach at Tel Baruch, because it is in the land, is sacred and that parts of Brooklyn or parts of Cincinnati because they are in the Diaspora are profane?

The reality of present-day Israel suggests something about the Land of Israel of the past, at least to the kind of Jews we are. We apply what we know about the present to what we wish to learn about the past; we think that history is without seams. As we read the Bible, we conclude that in that period, in the Land, were prophets and priests, those spiritual geniuses who created the Book of Books; and also people, people in all their complexity, some good, some bad, some saints, some sinners. The holiness of the land did not magically transform all upon it. Had it done so, much of what the prophets wrote would not have been written. There would have been no need to berate "those at ease in Zion"![2] We make the same assumptions about the period of the Mishnah: great rabbis and great sinners were living on the Land. Its soil was no magic panacea. From the Mishnaic period to the present, the land has had its share of spiritual giants and of lesser folk. We rejoice over the existence of the former, but we have to note the latter.

That being the case, upon what basis can we make the claim that the Land is sacred? Upon what basis could one deem a certain place profane? These questions become all the more difficult to answer, when, toward the end of the twentieth century, we ask ourselves, in every sense of the words, where we are. As Jews we are part of the past and its thought patterns; as moderns we are part of the present and its thought patterns. It is this "halting between two opinions" that is the problem and the glory of Liberal Judaism! We can read statements (and indeed we shall be quoting them) from the biblical period, the rabbinic period, and the medieval period, and we may ask ourselves whether the conceptual systems that created the notions of the sacred and the profane in the past still operate for us now. The past could look at a particular place, the Land of Israel, as the land that God had promised them. Its sanctity was therefore a function of a Divine act. Alas, our generation has lost much of its belief in such operation of the Divine. And yet here we are, in the Land, bound to Israel as a place and as a state in a way that goes beyond what many of us are able to articulate. Who can look at the origins of *Medinat Yisrael* and not see *etzba elohim?* So we believe even as we doubt, and we doubt even as we believe!

We shall approach the linked questions of the Land of Israel and the sacred, the Diaspora and the profane, by looking at certain texts in their original contexts and how later tradition dealt with them. We shall see that there is no clear equation of "the Land with the Sacred" or of "the Diaspora with the Profane." The reality of the Jewish people living inside and outside the Land and the fact that the documents of the Jewish people were composed inside and outside the Land preclude such a facile pairing.

It may be that "it is hardly an exaggeration to assert that Zion is the central theme of the Bible."[3] It is also true that the great formative experience of the Jewish people, at least as related by the Bible, the Revelation at Sinai, occurred *outside* the Land. The Giving of the Torah occurred outside the Land. The Mechilta even explains why the Torah was not given in the Land:

> The Torah was given in public, openly in a free place. For if the Torah had been given in the land of Israel, the Israelites could have said to the nations of the world: You have no share in it.[4]

The Mechilta passage suggests a shifting sense of what is sacred for Rabbinic Judaism: it is Torah more than the Land. Such a view would change, as we shall see, however, under changing circumstances. For the biblical writer, the Land was sacred because there was a threefold connection between God, the Jewish people, and the Land. Abraham, the progenitor of that people, was called to go "to the Land which I will show you."[5]

Thus, the biblical author writing in the Land much after Abraham made the connection of God, people, and Land. This threefold connection can be seen in David's complaint to Saul,

For they have driven me out this day that I should not cleave unto the inheritance of the Lord, saying: Go, serve other gods.[6]

It follows from this connection that if the people are false to their God they will lose their Land. Later rabbinic tradition, commenting on the linkage of land, people, and God, would say that the Land of Israel was a conditional gift dependant on the behavior of the People Israel.[7]

As a Divine Gift, the Land, for the biblical authors, had qualities that were magical. The waters of its Jordan River could cure the leprosy of a Syrian general. His response was twofold: he acknowledged the God of Israel, and he asked for two mules' burden of earth upon which he would henceforth worship that God. So for the biblical writer, it was the God of Israel and the Land of Israel in its most literal sense that were linked.[8]

Though we find the term *admat kodesh,* "holy ground," in the story of the Burning Bush,[9] an event that occurred outside of the Land, the Land itself receives that name in a prophetic promise of restoration: "And the Lord shall inherit Judah as His portion in the holy land *(al admat hakodesh)* and shall choose Jerusalem again."[10]

If the Land was holy, it followed for some that the land outside was not; in a prophetic curse, we learn that that land was unclean. Thus, Amos warned Amaziah that he would die upon "unclean land" *(adamah temayah)* when all of Israel would be exiled from its land.[11]

The curse was fulfilled at a later time when Israel was exiled to Babylon. The Psalmist wondered how he could sing God's song on foreign soil *(admat nechar);* nonetheless, in time a thriving Jewish community developed in Babylon while a Jewish community remained in the Land. The two communities gradually began to contend for hegemony. It seems that the fortunes of the emperical structures in which each was set ultimately determined which one succeeded.

The period of the Mishnah reflected a return to the importance of the Land; thus we learn that "There are ten degrees of holiness. The Land of Israel is holier than any other land."[12]

The period of the Gemara presented problems in the relation of the Land to Babylon. We read of a discussion of the last Mishnah in *Ketubot* 11:11: "[A man] may compel all [his household] to go up [with him] to the Land of Israel, but none may be compelled to leave it...."[13]

The Gemara quotes a Baraita that the compulsion spoken of relates to the unwilling spouse of a husband or a wife wishing to go to the land. If the recalcitrant spouse be the wife, she may be divorced without the payment of the *ketubah;* if it be the husband, he must divorce and pay the *ketubah.*[14]

Another Baraita is quoted that suggests the sacred quality of the Land:

> Our Rabbis taught: One should always live in the Land of Israel, even in a town most of whose inhabi-

tants are idolaters, but let no one live outside the Land, even in a town most of whose inhabitants are Israelites, for whoever lives outside the Land of Israel may be considered to have no God. For it is said in Scripture, "To give you the Land of Canaan, to be your God" (Lev. 25:38). Has he, then, the one who does not live in the Land, no God? But [this is what the text intended] to tell you, that whoever lives outside the Land may be regarded as one who worships idols. Similarly, it is said in Scripture in [the story of David], "For they have driven me but this day that I should not cleave to the inheritance of the Lord, saying: Go serve other gods" (I Sam. 26:19). Now, whoever said to David, 'Serve other gods'? But [the text intended] to tell you that whoever lives outside the Land may be regarded as one who worships idols.[15]

We should note the use of the verse from I Samuel as a proof text. It will reappear in a medieval commentary. By definition, a Baraita is a Tannaitic source that probably originated in the Land; it is found in a later Amoraic passage; here it is in the Babylonian Talmud. One would not think that the view that life outside the Land is life without God would originate outside the Land! The Baraita suggests something about the demographics of the time: there were towns in the Land filled with non-Jews and there were towns outside the Land filled with Jews. According to the view expressed, the presence of a large population of non-Jews did not affect the sacred status of the Land any more than the presence of a large population of Jews affected the nonsacred status of the areas outside the Land. The statement about having no God is softened (!?) a bit by comparing such a state to worshiping idols!

One can see in this exaggerated statement a response of part of the Palestinian community to the reality of the Jewish community in Babylon, yet the very next passage in the Gemara suggests a counterargument:

> Rabbi Zera was evading Rab Judah because he desired to go up to the Land of Israel while Rab Judah had expressed [the following view:] Whoever goes up from Babylon to the Land of Israel transgresses a positive commandment, for it is said in Scripture, "They shall be carried to Babylon, and there they shall be, until the day that I remember them, saith the Lord."[16]

Transgressing a positive commandment was no small matter! At a later point in the discussion, Rab Judah argued for the equivalence of Babylon and the Land of Israel:

> Whoever lives in Babylon is accounted as though he lived in the Land of Israel, for it is said in Scripture, "Ho, Zion, escape, thou that dwellest with the daughter of Babylon" (Zech. 2:11).[17]

It would seem, then, that for Rav Judah, Babylon took on some of the sanctity of the Land; he was quoted as saying: "As it is forbidden to leave the Land of Israel for Babylon, so it is forbidden to leave Babylon for other countries."[18]

ISRAEL AND THE DIASPORA

Leaving this life whether from Israel or from Babylon was also discussed:

> Rabbi Anan said, "Whoever is buried in the Land is deemed to be buried under the altar, since in respect to the latter it is written in Scripture, 'An altar of earth shalt thou make unto me' (Exod. 20:21), and in respect of the former it is written in Scripture, 'And his land doth make expiation for his people'" (Deut. 32:43).[19]

Surely, the notion that the Land itself makes expiation for sin suggests that it possesses a quality of holiness found nowhere else. Even were the modern reader to say that the passage exaggerates the impact of the Land on the religious consciousness of Jews, that reader could not deny the practice extending to the present of generations of Jews wishing to be buried in the Land even if they have lived their lives outside the Land. The next passage deals with that practice:

> Ulla was in the habit of paying visits to the Land of Israel but came to his eternal rest outside the Land. [When people] came and reported this to Rabbi Eleazar, he exclaimed, "Thou, Ulla, shouldst die in an unclean land" (Amos 7:17). "His coffin," they said to him, "has arrived." "Receiving a man in his lifetime," he replied, "is not the same as receiving him after his death."[20]

As with life in this world, so with life in the next; the Land of Israel figured in the question of who would or would not be resurrected:

> Rabbi Eleazar stated: the dead outside the Land will not be resurrected, for it is said in Scripture, "And I will set glory in the land of the living [implying] the dead of the land in which I have my desire will be resurrected, but the dead [of the land] in which I have no desire will not be resurrected."[21]

The question of resurrection for those buried outside the Land was finally resolved; they would require some problematic transportation:

> The righteous outside the Land...[will be revived] by rolling [to the Land of Israel]. Rabbi Abba Sala the Great demurred: "Will not the rolling be painful to the righteous?" Abaye replied: "Cavities will be made for them underground."[22]

Another sage thought that the Land itself and not the righteousness of the individual guaranteed survival after death, for

> Rabbi Jeremiah B. Abba [said] in the name of Rabbi Jochanan that whoever walks four cubits in the Land of Israel is assured a place in the world to come.[23]

Still another sage held that merely to live in the Land provided perduration even for a non-Jew:

> Even a Canaanite bondwoman who lives in the Land of Israel is assured a place in the world to come....[24]

So the Land is remarkable; it is a land flowing with sanctity: living there makes you free of sin;[25] walking there assures you of the world to come; being buried there expiates your sins; in life and in death, there could be no better place to be in than the Land of Israel! And yet the Jewish community dwelt in Babylon and lived very well. It did not drop all that it had and make *aliyah!* An aggadic interpretation of a verse from the Song of Songs provided reasons why Jews need not and, indeed, should not leave for the Land. From "I adjure you, O daughters of Jerusalem, by the gazelles, and by the hinds of the field, that you waken not, nor stir up love till it please" (Song 2:7). Rav Judah (of whom we have already heard) and others developed the notion that the three adjurations in the verse suggested

> One, that Israel shall not go up [all together as if surrounded] by a wall; the second, that...Israel ...shall not rebel against the nations of the world, and the third...the Holy One...adjured the idolaters that they shall not oppress Israel too much....[26]

As later Jewish history was to teach, the last adjuration, directed to the nations of the world, was, alas, not always heard. Still, this interpretation of the Song of Songs did provide (and still provides for some) justification for remaining outside the Land.

Subsequent Jewish history provided examples of Jews living inside and outside the Land. Whatever its sanctity, the Land could not guarantee that the Jewish community within its borders would have dominion over the Jewish communities of the Diaspora even as Ben Meir's controversy with Saadia should remind us.[27] For Saadia, it was not the Land and its sacred nature that provided the elements of Jewish identity. In a passage that has become well known, he said,

> Our nation of the children of Israel is a nation only by virtue of its laws. Since, then, the Creator has stated that the Jewish nation was destined to exist as long as heaven and earth would exist, its laws would, of necessity, have to endure as long as would heaven and earth.[28]

Most of the Jewish people were in the Diaspora, not in the Land. The Diaspora made possible the cultural interchange that brought in the new intellectual current of philosophy that washed over the Jewish community. Even so, the Land played a crucial role in the thought of Jehudah Halevi (1080-1141). The Land of Israel makes prophecy possible; because the People of Israel are not in the Land, prophecy is not found among them. As grapes on vines depend on the soil of the vineyard, so the development of the Children of Israel depends on the Land of Israel. In its way this is a natural phenomenon, for

> There are places in which particular plants, metals, or animals are found, or where the inhabitants are distinguished by their form and character, since perfection or deficiency of the soul are produced by the mingling of the elements.[29]

The Land has such perfection that it can generate prophecy even outside its borders, for, "Whosoever prophesied did so either in the [Holy] Land, or concerning it...."[30]

One might say that Halevi's "naturalistic" approach to prophecy makes the Land for him, if not *kadosh* in the sense of "sacred," certainly *kadosh* in the sense of "special"! Halevi accepted the special quality that the Rabbis had noted about the Land, since he quoted a number of passages from the Talmud in praise of it, particularly the passage from *Ketubot* 111a.[31]

Legend has it that Halevi acted upon his views of the Land, made a pilgrimage to it, and died there, supposedly with his last breath reciting his ode to Zion.[32]

Another who alluded to the same Talmudic passage and who later acted on his belief that the Land had a particular sanctity was the Biblical commentator Nahmanides (1195-1270). He took the injunction "And ye shall drive out the inhabitants of the land and dwell therein" (Num. 33:53) as a positive commandment. He found support in the aforementioned Talmudic passage that insisted that a man might force his wife to go up to the Land.[33] Others—Rashi, for example—drew a different conclusion from the verse, because they lived and remained outside the Land.[34] Even so, they created their own sacred places *chutz l'aaretz:* the *bet haknesset* and the *bet hamidrash*. Maimonides' exposition of the sanctity of a synagogue and the study house is most instructive. We read that

> Even though synagogues [*batai kenaysiot*] and study houses [*batai midrashot*] may be in ruins, their

sanctity remains, as it is written, "And I will bring your sanctuaries into desolation"[35] (Lev. 26:31).

The use of the biblical verse reminds the reader of the parallel passage in the Mishnah:

> Moreover, Rabbi Judah said: [Even] if a synagogue was in ruins lamentation for the dead may not be made therein, nor may they...make of it a short by-path; for it is written, "And I will bring your sanctuaries into desolation" (Lev. 26:31)—their sanctity [endures] although they lie desolate.[36]

Now, the Torah verse Rabbi Judah and Maimonides used as a proof text referred to the Land; the synagogue of which Rabbi Judah spoke was in the Land; and the synagogue and the study house of which Maimonides spoke were not in the Land. By a kind of algebraic equation of sanctity, what had been a sanctuary and a place of sanctity in the Land were now transferred outside the Land. The synagogue and the study hall became the sacred substitutes for the Land. The Land remained within them even if they had not remained in the Land. In them, Hebrew, the language of the Land, was heard; in them, books linked to the Land were read; and in them, the calendar of the Land shaped Jewish experience. Outside the Land, in these structures, one prayed that the wind might blow and that rain might fall—in the Land! Three times a year, on the pilgrim festivals, one heard that to be outside the Land was fit punishment for sins committed inside the Land! One prayed to be returned with all other exiles that were to be returned to the Land. With all this, one might look at the *bet haknesset* and the *bet hamidrash* as places of extraterritorial identity, as if somehow they were Land of Israel embassies. It may be that, on an unconscious level, the present custom in synagogues the world over of having an Israeli flag on the *bimah* is an acting out of the notion that wherever we may be as Jews, we sense that our connection to the sacred is somehow related to the Land of Israel.

We Jews are in the Land and outside the Land. We seek the sacred in both places. We would flee from the profane in both places. We are connected to the Land in ways we cannot express, whether we live in it or merely visit it. The Land is part of the Jewish memory bank; without it, we could not be Jews. "It is more sacred than any other!" The vision of what life could be was first formed here. It is the task of Jews living here and living *chutz l'aaretz* to make that vision real here and wherever we live. Then the Land of Israel will truly be sacred and so will the Diaspora.

Notes

1. Psalm 137:3, 4. Note the linking of God, Zion, and people: *aych nashir,* "How shall we sing"!

2. Amos 6:1.

3. Abraham S. Halkin, "Zion in Biblical Literature," in *Zion in Jewish Literature,* edited by Abraham S. Halkin, Brown Classics in Judaica (Lanham, MD: University Press, 1988), pp. 18–37.

4. *Mechilta, Tractate Bahodesh; Mekilta de Rabbi Ishmael: A Critical Edition on the Basis of the Manuscripts and Early Editions with an English Translation,* Introduction and Notes by Jacob Z. Lauterbach, Vol. 2 (Philadelphia: Jewish Publication Society, 1949), p. 198. Henceforth cited as Mekilta: Vol 2: p. 198. The Mechilta in Tractate Amalek will tell the reader that: "Three things were given conditionally: the Land of Israel, the Temple, and the kingdom of David." Mekilta: Vol. 2, p. 188.

5. Genesis 12:1.

6. 1 Samuel 26:19.

7. Mekilta, Vol. 2, p. 188.

8. 2 Kings 5:15ff.

9. Exodus 3:5.

10. Zechariah 2:16.

11. Amos 7:17.

12. *Mishnah Kelim* 6:1, *The Mishnah*, Translated by Herbert C. Danby (Oxford: Oxford University Press, 1948), p. 605. Henceforth cited as Danby. Bartinoro (ad locum) reminds us that the Mishnaic statement is related to the earlier statement in the passage about different levels of uncleanliness.

13. *Ketubot* 110b; *Hebrew-English Edition of The Babylonian Talmud: Ketuboth*, Translated into English with Notes, Glossary, and Indexes by Rabbi Dr. H. Freedman and under the Editorship of Rabbi Dr. I. Epstein (London: Soncino Press, 1967), p. 709. Henceforth cited in this manner: *Ketubot* 110b; S, p. 709.

14. Ibid.

15. Ibid, S. p. 712.

16. Ibid., *Ketubot* 110b, 110a; S, pp. 712, 713.

17. Ibid., *Ketubot* 111a, S, p. 715.

18. Ibid., S, pp. 714, 715.

19. Ibid.

20. Ibid. Note the use again of Amos 7:17.

21. Ibid., *Ketubot* 111a, S, p. 716.

22. Ibid.

23. Ibid., S.p. 717.

24. Ibid.

25. Ibid., S. p. 714.

26. Ibid., *Ketubot* 111a p. 713.

ISRAEL AND THE DIASPORA

27. Cf. *Jewish Encyclopedia,* entry on Saadia, Vol. 10, p. 679.

28. Saadia Gaon, *The Book of Beliefs and Opinions,* Translated from the Arabic and the Hebrew by Samuel Rosenblat (New Haven: Yale University Press, 1948), Treatise Three: Command and Prohibition, Chap. 8, p. 158.

29. Judah Halevi, *The Book of Kuzari,* translated from the Arabic by Hartwig Hirschfeld (New York: Pardes Publishing House, 1946), Part Two, 10, p. 77. Henceforth cited in this manner: *Kuzari* II:10, p. 77.

30. *Kuzari* II:14, p. 78.

31. *Kuzari* II:22, pp. 85, 86.

32. Israel Zinburg, *Toldot Sifrut Yisrael,* Vol. 1, p. 115.

33. In his commment on Num. 33:53.

34. Rashi on Num. 33:53.

35. Moses Maimonides, *Mishneh Torah, Hilchot Tefillah,* Chapter 11:11.

36. *Mishnah Megillah* 3:3. Danby, p. 205.

THE LAND, THE LAW, AND THE LIBERAL CONSCIENCE

John D. Rayner

For some years now the question has been hotly debated whether it is right that, for the sake of peace, the State of Israel should be prepared to relinquish some of the territories now under its control. The assassination of Prime Minister Yitzchak Rabin on November 4, 1995, motivated by fanatical opposition to a peace process involving acceptance of that principle, has brought the issue into sharp and tragic focus.

Not only is it the main issue dividing Israel's political parties, but, as the background of the assassin has highlighted, it is also a matter of religious controversy. But the religious debate has been conducted mainly among Orthodox rabbis;[1] there have been few contributions from exponents of Progressive Judaism.[2] This absence of a Progressive voice is unfortunate, for it leaves the field to the Orthodox—apart from the secular, who are themselves divided on the issue—and obscures the fact that there is an alternative religious view.

THE ORTHODOX APPROACH

From an Orthodox point of view, the Hebrew Bible, as interpreted in the rabbinic tradition, is divinely authoritative both in its totality and in every particular. Sometimes, admittedly, it is not immediately clear what it means; hence the qualification "as interpreted." And sometimes the interpreters themselves are not completely in agreement; hence the *gedoley ha-dor* (preeminent exponents of the tradition in each generation) may incline toward one *shitah* (school of thought) or another, or even offer their own *chiddush* (innovative interpretation). Thus, there is *some* room for maneuver, but not much; for all essentials were long ago definitively settled. There is certainly never any question but that whatever Scripture says concerning God's promises and commandments, once its correct interpretation has been determined, is to be believed and obeyed.

Furthermore—and this is crucial to our inquiry—the Hebrew Bible, as correctly interpreted, is the *sole* authority for all questions of conduct, both in matters of ritual and in matters of ethics. Indeed, the difference between these two spheres is barely recognized. Admittedly, the tradition speaks of *mitzvot she-beyn adam la-Makom* (duties to God) and *mitzvot she-beyn adam la-chavero* (duties to fellow human beings), but little is made of the distinction. As there are right and wrong ways of treating employees, so there are right and wrong ways of waving a *lulav;* and there is little hint of any awareness that in the two instances "right" and "wrong" are used in fundamentally different senses. In both cases, what is right is what the *halakhah* enjoins and what is wrong is what the *halakhah* forbids. There is no ethic independent of the *halakhah*.[3]

THE PROGRESSIVE APPROACH

Progressive Judaism's understanding is altogether different. At least that is true of the liberal tendency within it. (Other, more conservative leanings, tend to fudge the issues.) According to this view, the Hebrew Bible is a literature spanning a thousand years and displaying both unity and diversity, the latter being manifest in a broad spectrum of literary styles and religious perceptions. Those who wrote it were not only human and therefore fallible, but also products of the sociocultural milieu of the ancient Near East in which they lived. They sometimes, nevertheless, expressed ideas far ahead of their times. In these we can legitimately see both the impact of revelation and inspiration and the working out of the implications of monotheism. Sometimes their thinking was on a level with what one finds in other contemporary civilizations and in no way remarkable; and in not a few instances it has been left behind by subsequent advances in Jewish or in human thought.

Furthermore, development is discernible in the diversity. This is, admittedly, not all unidirectional; for there are ups and downs. But on the whole the monotheism becomes more categorical, the ethical consciousness more humane, and the conception of Israel's role in human history more universal; and when one encounters evidence of retrogression, it takes only a little discernment to recognize it for what it is.

Therefore, too, the Bible as a whole is only a stage—albeit the first and grandest stage—in the historical development of Judaism. Rabbinic Judaism shows many advances, of which the change from Temple sacrifice to synagogue prayer is the most obvious; and there have been advances since the Talmud, such as the prohibition of polygamy.

Above all, the liberal approach to the Bible and likewise to its rabbinic interpretation, rests on the conviction that there are universal ethical principles by which we can evaluate particular teachings of the tradition. These principles derive in large measure from the tradition itself, but not in the simplistic sense that we accept them on its authority. Rather, we affirm them because, as beings endowed by God with a capacity for ethical cognition, we can see for ourselves that they are true. Where the tradition speaks with different voices, it is the same ethical cognition that enables us to discern the higher from the lower. We may occasionally be able to advance beyond the tradition by extrapolating tendencies that are discernible but incomplete within it. The raising of the status of women to one of equality with men is an example of that.

Progressive Judaism, therefore, views the tradition historically and, though with all due reverence, critically, evaluating it by the criteria of an ethical conscience that, though largely nurtured by the tradition, is nevertheless independent of it.

SCRIPTURAL PROMISES

The Hebrew Bible is replete with passages that affirm a unique bond between the Jewish people and a particular territory that is at first referred to as the land of Canaan and later by various other terms, including *Eretz Yisrael,* the Land of Israel. (The latter occurs only rarely in the Bible, e.g., Ezek. 40:2, but is the regular designation of the country in postbiblical Jewish literature, from the Mishnah onward.) In Roman times and subsequently it became known as Palestine. Each of these names prejudges issues that have yet to be discussed. We shall therefore call it simply "the Land."

Many of the passages in question are in the nature of divine promises to Abraham (Gen. 12:2, 13:15, 15:7, 18, 17:8), Isaac (Gen. 26:3), Jacob (Gen. 28:13, 35:12, 48:4), Moses (Exod. 3:8, 6:8; Num. 33:53, 34:2; Deut. 11:24), and Joshua (Josh. 1:3). Some of them go on to define the borders of the Land, a subject to which we shall return. Several include the phrase, "To you do I give it, and to your seed, for ever," which is a legal formula known from other ancient Near Eastern texts.

Some of these promises occur in the specific context of the Covenant (Gen. 15:18, 17:7), suggesting the possibility that if the people fail to fulfill their Covenantal obligations, they may forfeit their title to the Land or be exiled from it. Sometimes that implication is spelled out—for example, "You shall keep My statutes and My ordinances...so that the land does not vomit you out, as it vomited out the nation that was before you" (Lev. 18:26ff; cf. Lev. 26:27-39, Jer. 18:7f). For the most part, however, the divine promises appear to be unconditional. Orthodox Judaism accordingly draws from them the inference that the Land "belongs" to the Jewish people, and to no other people, in perpetuity.

A liberal view would acknowledge that as what the writers of the Bible believed, but it would try to understand that belief in its historical context. One aspect of this is the notion, common in the ancient Near East, of territorial deities; another is the need to reconcile that notion with the monotheistic idea. The argument, we must imagine, ran as follows: on the one hand God is the Owner of all lands, for "[t]he earth is God's and all its fullness" (Ps. 24:1). On the other hand God is the Owner of *the* Land in a special sense, calling it "My land" (Joel 4:2) and keeping it under constant surveillance (Deut. 11:12). The solution of the paradox is that God, at an early time, parceled out the earth to its various peoples, assigning the choicest land to the chosen people (Deut. 32:8). This idea should also be seen in the context of the etiological motif—the desire to explain, often fancifully, how things came to be as they are—which features so prominently in the Bible.

Because our ancestors believed what they did, it doesn't follow that they were right. Surely, it would be theologically naive to suppose that God "gave" the Land to them in any straightforward sense. It is, indeed, entirely credible that their settlement in the Land for the purpose of creating in it a monotheistic society would have accorded with the Divine Will. But the means by which they are said to have appropriated it, involving genocidal war against its inhabitants, raises serious questions, to which we shall return.

The further assertion that the Land was given to the Jewish people in perpetuity raises still other difficulties, for the biblical writers had no means of knowing what God's long-term geopolitical plans were, nor indeed could there have been such if human free will is a fact. Because of that fact, as we have seen, the Israelites might conceivably forfeit their moral title to the Land; and because of the same fact there are, in the course of history, conquests and migrations that may materially alter the factors relevant to a just land distribution.

In addition, we have to reckon with the possibility that although it was God's intention that the Jewish people grow up in the Land, it was not God's intention that they remain confined within it forever. This view can draw support from statements in the classical sources of Judaism that see positive value in the Diaspora—for instance, that "God scattered Israel among the nations for the sole purpose that proselytes should become numerous among them."[4] It is also a view that progressive Jewish thinkers have strongly held in the past, as in this prayer: "Enlighten all that call themselves by Thy name with the knowledge that the sanctuary of wood and stone which once crowned Zion's hill was but a gate, through which Israel stepped out into the world to lead mankind nearer unto Thee."[5] Today, most Progressive Jews would wish to qualify that by stressing the positive value of the rebirth of Israel in its ancient homeland but without therefore negating the Diaspora.

JOHN D. RAYNER

It would certainly be consistent with a liberal Jewish theology to believe that it was God's will not only that the Jewish people grow up in the Land, but that they maintain their love for it and, whenever conditions permit, live in it, cultivate it, and establish in it the most flourishing possible Jewish communal life. To invoke alleged divine promises contained in ancient Hebrew literature as a ground for claiming present ownership of the Land, in disregard of all other considerations, however, is not an option open to nonfundamentalists.

THE "HOLINESS" OF THE LAND

In addition to divine promises of the Land, the Bible abounds in praises of it. It is said to be "a land flowing with milk and honey" (Exod. 13:5); "a good land, with streams and springs and fountains issuing from plain and hill; a land of wheat and barley, of vines, figs and pomegranates ... a land where you may eat bread without scarcity, where you will lack nothing" (Deut. 8:7ff); "the most beautiful of all lands" (Ezek. 20:6, 15); and so forth. These eulogies, which continue in the rabbinic *aggadah* and in subsequent Jewish literature, not least in the poetry of Judah Halevi, are authentic expressions of a love for the Land that Jews have felt throughout their history and that requires no apology.

More difficult is the concept of the "holiness" of the Land *(kedushat ha-aretz)*. As a matter of fact, the term "Holy Land" is more commonly used by Christians than by Jews. One of its Hebrew equivalents, *admat ha-kodesh,* is found in that sense only once in the Bible (Zech. 2:16); another, *eretz ha-kodesh,* is first found in medieval sources. Nevertheless, the underlying idea is implied in the Bible and spelled out in rabbinic literature. "The

Land of Israel," says the Mishnah, "is the holiest of all lands."[6] Admittedly, the term is used there in a technical-legal sense, the issue being the provenance of agricultural produce for the purpose of various kinds of Temple offerings.

A leading Anglo-Jewish scholar, Hyam Maccoby, has written: "The Land of Israel was indeed regarded as holy in various halakhic ways, but this territorial holiness is not a mystical value in Judaism."[7] Nevertheless, the concept of holiness as a quality that in some supernatural way inheres in the Land does seem to be implied in the disqualification of other lands for cultic purposes. A number of aggadic statements hold likewise (for instance, that "the very air of the Land of Israel makes wise"[8]; that "those who live in the Land of Israel are as if they had a God, whereas those who live outside the Land of Israel are as if they had no God"[9]; that "those who live in the Land of Israel live without sin"[10]; and that, "once the Land of Israel had been chosen, all other lands were excluded from divine revelations"[11]).

At any rate, insofar as such a "mystical" concept is to be found in Jewish tradition, it must be repudiated from a liberal point of view, for it is clearly incompatible with the Omnipresence of God, which is a necessary corollary of monotheism, and it obscures an essential distinction: between the holiness of God, which is primary, and the "holiness" of things, persons, places, and times associated with God, which is only a "reflected" holiness, and therefore secondary. The Land, of course, has many "holy" associations for Progressives, as for all Jews, but they would deem it all the more important, nevertheless, to emphasize that "the Eternal One is great beyond the borders of Israel" (Mal. 1:5).

JOHN D. RAYNER

THE BORDERS OF THE LAND

The question of the "holiness" of the Land is closely related to that of its borders, for it is only within these that its "holiness" is said to reside, and from that distinction a number of legal consequences follow for the so-called *mitzvot ha-teluyot ba-aretz* (commandments dependent on the Land). Most of these relate to the Temple, the monarchy, and agriculture and do not concern us here; but one or two related *mitzvot* concerning settlement in the Land are relevant to our inquiry, and we shall return to them.

There is no simple answer to the question of borders, however, for they were variously conceived in different periods, depending partly on the actual extent of Israel's territorial control at the time and partly on the writer's idealizing imagination. Within the biblical period it is customary to distinguish three stages associated respectively with Abraham, Joshua, and Ezra.

The divine promise to Abraham reads: "To your descendants I give this land, from the river of Egypt to the great river, the river Euphrates, the land of the Kenites, the Kenizzites, the Kadmonites, the Hittites, the Perizzites, the Rephaim, the Amorites, the Canaanites, the Girgashites, and the Jebusites" (Gen. 15:18-21). This, the most extensive definition, is regarded as an idealistic one that will be fully realized only in the messianic age. In that sense it is reiterated elsewhere: for instance, "I will set your borders from the Red Sea to the sea of the Philistines, and from the wilderness to the Euphrates" (Exod. 23:31) and, "Every place on which you set foot shall be yours; your territory shall extend from the wilderness to the Lebanon and from the river, the river Euphrates, to the Western sea" (Deut. 11:24; cf. Josh. 1:4).

Considerably more modest in extent is the territory that the generation of the Exodus is promised through Moses and subsequently occupies—in large part though not entirely—under the leadership of Joshua. This is defined in great detail in Numbers (34:1-13) and Joshua (12:1-6, 13:1-7). Similar references can be found in Ezekiel (47:15-20). It is largely bounded by the Mediterranean in the west and the Jordan in the east, but spreads some way toward Egypt in the southwest and into Syria in the northeast. This area, insofar as it was conquered under Joshua, is said to have acquired by virtue of that fact a "first sanctification" *(kedushah rishonah)*. According to many authorities, however, this conferred on it only a temporary "holiness," for what is gained by conquest can be lost by conquest.[12]

Even less extensive (perhaps stretching from Akko in the north to Ashkelon in the south) was the area occupied by the Jewish exiles who returned from Babylonia following the decree of Cyrus, king of Persia, and in the days of Ezra. This area is said to have acquired a "second sanctification" *(kedushah sheniyyah)*. According to some authorities, that, too, lapsed after the Dispersion; according to others, perhaps because it resulted from a never-rescinded royal decree, it has remained in force ever since.[13]

The foregoing is only a simplified summary. In fact, the question of the borders of the Land is a great deal more complicated, both from a *halakhic* and from a historical point of view.[14] In the words of a contemporary Israeli Orthodox rabbi:

> There is a great discrepancy between the actual borders of the Land of Canaan at the time of Abraham (Gen. 10:19), concerning which it is said:

"to your seed have I given this land...." and the Land promised by God to Abraham (Gen. 15:18-21). Both outlines differ from the boundary promised to Israel in the wilderness (Exod. 23:31) and the promise made before their entry into the Land (Deut. 1:7, 32:2-4). Moreover, all the Biblical borders differ from what was to be the ideal future boundary (Ezek. 47:13). Then, again, all the aforesaid borders were not identical with the Land actually divided up between the twelve Tribes by lot (Num. 34:2-12). Furthermore, the areas thus divided did not tally with the "inheritance" and "settlement" in the days of Joshua and the Judges (Josh. 12, 13; Judges 3:4), which, again, differed from the "second inheritance" during the days of Ezra and Nehemia, King Yannai and Agrippas I.[15]

We need not pursue these complications any further, however, for we shall argue that the precise nature of the various ancient borders has no relevance to the contemporary territorial question that concerns us.

JEWISH SETTLEMENT

The Bible devotes much attention to the manner in which, by various stages, the Israelites entered the Land, settled in it, and gained possession of it. In the period of the Patriarchs the process is depicted as a largely peaceful one, involving migrations (Gen. 12:1-6), treaties (Gen. 21:22-34, 26:26-31) and purchases (Gen. 23:3-20, Gen. 33:19). By contrast, the occupation of the Land under Joshua involved violent conflict with its established inhabitants.

THE LAND, THE LAW, AND THE LIBERAL CONSCIENCE

As related in the Bible, it was nevertheless carried out in response to divine exhortations. Here are some of the key passages:

> The Eternal One spoke to Moses in the plains of Moab by the Jordan near Jericho, saying, "Speak to the children of Israel and say to them: When you cross over the Jordan into the land of Canaan, you shall drive out [*ve-horashtem*] all the inhabitants of the land from before you.... You shall take possession of the land, and settle in it [*vishavtem bah*], for I have given the land to you to possess" (Num. 33:52). "When the Eternal One your God brings you into the land which you are about to enter and possess, and casts out many nations before you—the Hittites, the Girgashites, the Amorites, the Canaanites, the Perizzites, the Hivites, and the Jebusites, seven nations mightier and more numerous than you—and when the Eternal One your God gives them over to you and you defeat them, then you shall utterly destroy them; you shall make no covenant with them and show them no mercy [*ve-lo techonnem*]" (Deut. 7:1,2). "For you are about to cross over the Jordan to go in to possess the land which the Eternal One your God is giving you; therefore take possession of it, and settle in it [*virishtem otah vishavtem bah*]" (Deut. 11:31). "When the Eternal One your God has cut off from before you the nations which you are to penetrate and dispossess, you shall dispossess them and settle in their land [*ve-yarashta otam v'yashavta be-artzam*]" (Deut. 12:29).

These passages raise an obvious difficulty: how can they be reconciled with the belief in a universal, just, and merciful God? We are presumably dealing here with an ex post facto justification of past events. In reality, the occupation was most probably effected not by one major campaign, as recounted in the book of Joshua, but by a series of minor incursions, and it is therefore legitimate to wonder whether it could have been effected by peaceful means.

But these are matters of academic speculation and of no contemporary relevance. So, at least, one might have thought. Because these passages contain a number of imperatives (which we have highlighted), however, the question arises from a *halakhic* point of view whether they were addressed only to the generation of the wilderness and then lapsed, or whether they remained in force. In other words, is there a continuing obligation upon Jews to settle and live in the Land?

The prevailing but not unanimous answer of the *halakhah* is yes. Rabbinic literature goes so far as to say that the *mitzvah* of living in the Land is as weighty as all the other *mitzvot* put together![16] Of the *Rishonim* (earlier authorities), the outstanding exponent of the view that the *mitzvah* remains in force was Nahmanides: "Rambam understands all the passages of the Torah instructing the Jewish People and Joshua to conquer, take possession, and settle the Land as being commands not addressed to that generation alone, but to all future generations."[17] Accordingly, he regarded it as a biblical law (*mi-de-oraita*), based on Num. 33:53 (see above), and criticized Maimonides for not including it in his compilation of the 613 commandments.[18]

Why Maimonides did not include the *mitzvah* has raised much speculation. According to the *Talmudic Encyclopedia,* he regarded it as having the force of only rabbinic (*mi-de-rabbanan*), not biblical law.[19] Rabbi David Bleich, however, writes:

> The simplest and most obvious reason for this omission is that Rambam does not view this injunction as constituting a mandatory obligation binding upon all generations. Rambam may well have deemed the commandment to have been binding only upon the generation of the wilderness to whom it was addressed and to those who were charged with the original conquest of the land of Canaan, but not intended as a binding commandment for all posterity. Alternatively, Rambam may have interpreted the verse as constituting sage counsel, as did Rashi, rather than a commandment. It thus follows that, in our time, according to Rambam, there is no divine imperative requiring a Jew to remove himself from the Diaspora and to establish residence in Israel.[20]

But he goes on to concede that "in the absence of Rambam's position one would be hard put to excuse failure to settle in Israel."[21]

Progressive Jews would be inclined to endorse the most liberal interpretation of Maimonides' opinion. There can be no question of an *obligation* on all Jews to settle in Israel. Of course, Progressive Judaism recognizes the unique opportunities and challenges that the State of Israel presents. Many Progressive Jews have indeed settled there, and Progressive Jewish organizations have endorsed the 1951 Jerusalem Programme of the World Zionist Organization, amended in 1956, with its call for "the ingathering of the Jewish people in its historic homeland *Eretz Yisrael* through *aliyah* from all countries," but with the explicit or implicit proviso that *aliyah* is only to be encouraged, not demanded; and on the understanding that Jewish life in the Diaspora also continues to have positive value.

THE RIGHTS OF NON-JEWS

We must now return to the negative side of the Bible's exhortations concerning the occupation of the Land: namely, its call for the expulsion, if not annihilation, of its indigenous population. We have already touched briefly on the moral difficulties this raises. Here we should like, additionally, to draw attention to an excellent discussion of the topic by Rabbi W. Gunther Plaut in his *Torah Commentary*,[22] where he points out, inter alia, that the injunction to annihilate the Canaanites was, as a matter of historical fact, never carried out, and that the passages in question, attributed to the age of Moses, need to be understood in the light of a much later struggle against Canaanite idolatry.

The question we nevertheless need to raise is whether these anti-Gentile injunctions play any role in postbiblical Jewish law; and here again the answer is, to some extent, yes.

We may indeed take it from Bleich that "there is, in our day, no obligation to wage war for conquest of *Eretz Yisrael* or for retention of sanctified territories, even according to the opinion of Rambam."[23] The fact is, however, that the modern State of Israel, as a result of a series of defensive wars, has gained control over extensive territories that include a large Palestinian-Arab population. Questions about the status of these and other non-Jewish residents cannot be avoided and have received attention from Orthodox rabbinic authorities according to their understanding of the *halakhah*.

The key verse here is Deut. 7:2, quoted above, and especially the phrase *lo techonnem,* which is usually translated "[Y]ou shall show them no mercy." The Talmud, however, already took the verb as coming not from the root *chanan,* "to have mercy," but from the root *chanah,* "to camp," interpreting it as a prohibition against the sale of real estate to non-Jews within the borders of the Land.[24]

That, one may think, is restrictive enough, but there are one or two further restrictions. When Jews are in control of the Land, says Maimonides,[25] they may not permit idolaters to live in it at all, except insofar as they undertake to observe the seven Noachide laws (which include the prohibition of idolatry), since it says, "They shall not live in your land" (Exod. 23:33). Seeing that Christians and Muslims have, since the Middle Ages, been considered monotheists in Jewish law, that should present no problem; yet there is a rigorous view that would require non-Jews claiming such status to make a formal declaration of allegiance to the Noachide laws before a rabbinical court![26]

Furthermore, since these prohibitions apply to all areas now under Israel's control that fall within the boundaries of the Land as *halakhically* defined, they could be, and have been, used as an argument against the surrender of any of the territories in question on the ground that such surrender would cause real estate that "belongs" to the Jewish people to fall into non-Jewish hands. Accordingly, an eminent Israeli Orthodox rabbi has stated that "the precept of *lo techonnem* certainly applies, and no part of *Eretz Yisrael* must on any account be handed over to non-Jews, whether individually or by the national authorities."[27]

TERRITORY AND PEACE

Such extreme views are held by much of the ultra-Orthodox leadership, both in Israel and in the Diaspora. Why that should be so is an interesting question. It is partly due, one presumes, to the rejection of history, reason, and any ethic independent of the *halakhah,* characteristic of that tendency. It also has something to do with its traditional negativism toward the whole culture of the Enlightenment and liberalism, but it has been intensified by a strong feeling, often amounting to a fervent conviction, that recent events—the rebirth of a Jewish state after 2,000 years, the War of Independence, the Six Day War, the Entebbe raid—betoken nothing less than *ikvey ha-mashiach* (the footsteps of the Messiah) and *atchalta di-ge'ullah* (the beginning of redemption). They are seen as triumphantly demonstrating God's power to fulfill ancient prophecies and thus as validating the fundamentalist reading of Scripture. To such an eschatological way of thinking, all things are possible, and ethical scruples may be suspended.

Those who share this mentality live in a dream world that has its own logic but bears no relation to any solid reality. They become natural allies of secular forms of ultranationalist fanaticism that are likewise disdainful of reason.

Thus, Rav Avraham Elkana Kahana-Shapira writes: "The very existence of a *mitzvah* to conquer *Eretz Yisrael* indicates that it is God's will that the whole of *Eretz Yisrael* should be in our possession."[28] Similarly, Rav Yakov Ariel (Shtiglitz), interpreting R. Yehoshua of Kotna's view of *Mitzvot Yishuv Ha'aretz* (the commandment to settle the Land), concludes: "Any form of withdrawal from the regained territories constitutes a negation of the *mitzvah* and a hindrance to the process of Redemption."[29]

One should not think, however, that all Orthodox rabbis, even of the "old school," take such a hawkish view. The former Sefardi Chief Rabbi of Israel, for instance, Ovadiah Yosef, holds that the *halakhic* arguments for the retention of all the conquered territories must give way before the following considerations: that peace is unattainable without territorial concession; that in the absence of peace, there will be more war and bloodshed; that *pikkuah nefesh* (saving human life) must be the overriding objective; and that it is for the political and military experts, not the rabbis, to judge what measures are best calculated to achieve that end.[30]

Similar views have been expressed by the former Chief Rabbi of the United Hebrew Congregations of the British Commonwealth, Lord (Immanuel) Jakobovits, and by his successor, Rabbi Dr. Jonathan Sacks. Hyam Maccoby summed up their position, which seems to be also his own, when he wrote that "the requirements of peace come before considerations of territory in rabbinic thinking. The holiness of the Land does not preclude the right of a Jewish ruling body to come to terms with an enemy in the interests of overall peace, even when such terms involve the ceding of a portion of the land categorized as holy."[31]

This line of argument is very powerful in view of Judaism's immense emphasis on the ideal of peace (e.g., "Seek peace, and pursue it," Psalm 34:15) as well as the *halakhic* principle that *pikkuah nefesh* takes priority over all other commandments except the prohibitions of idolatry, incest, and murder.[32]

Unfortunately, however, the argument is not unassailable, for one can contend that since war by its very nature involves casualties, the principle of *pikkuah nefesh* does not apply to it, and that since any war that may be necessary to defend the conquered territories would be in the nature of *milchemet mitzvah* (obligatory war), the risk involved must be taken.

Thus, Rav Shlomo Aviner quotes Rav Avraham Kook as follows:

> All activities designed to transfer ownership of parts of *Eretz Yisrael* from the hands of gentiles to those of Jews come within the definition of the Divine commandment to conquer the Land of Israel, outweighing all the commandments of the Torah. This is borne out by the fact that by definition the Torah obliges us to implement this precept even to the point of war, which naturally entails risking the loss of life.[33]

Similarly, Rav Yehoshuah Menachem Ehrenberg writes: "Since the Torah obliges us to conquer *Eretz Yisrael* with all the danger to life that this involves, how can we justify giving up territory that we have already conquered because of *pikkuah nefesh*.[34] And Rav Avraham Elkana Kahana-Shapira makes it clear that according to his interpretation of Maimonides, "wars of conquest in the Holyland [*sic*]—at all times—fall into the category of *milchamot mitzvah.*"[35]

SUMMARY OF THE ORTHODOX POSITION

The Orthodox position, as we have seen, is not monolithic. There is fundamental agreement, however, that divine promises of the Hebrew Bible are to be taken at face value; that the Land, whatever may be its precise extent, is, within those limits, holy; that de jure it belongs to the Jewish people, and to no other, forever; and that in the messianic age, the imminent approach of which we may or may not be witnessing in our time, it will be so de facto.

Thus, the Jewish people's claim to the Land is grounded in the Divine Will as revealed in Scripture, a point commonly reinforced by reference to Rashi's comment on the first verse of Genesis, where he asks why the Bible begins with the creation of the world and, quoting Psalm 111:6, replies: "So that, if the nations were to say to Israel, 'You are robbers, because you conquered the seven nations of Canaan,' they may be able to reply, "The whole earth belongs to God, who created it and gave it to whomever He thought fit; by His will He gave it to the seven nations, and by His will He took it from them and gave it to us.'"

Beyond that basic principle there is divergence, particularly on the rights of non-Jews in the Land and the question of whether it is permissible to relinquish some portions of it for the sake of peace. Some authorities believe that in furtherance of the Divine Plan, the non-Jewish population of the Land should be kept as low as possible and their rights of residence subject to stringent conditions. Thus, Professor Yehudah Elizur writes: "This, then, is the message and iron rule of the Bible, that no people can ever strike roots in *Eretz Yisrael*, the Land awaiting the homecoming of its sons and daughters."[36] And, interpreting Nahmanides, he continues: "Israel and the Land of Israel belong to one another; when united, both flourish and are blessed. The converse is true when Land and people are separated; then misfortune takes hold of both, Israel turning into a wasteland and the Jews suffering persecution, exile and migration from one place to another."[37]

Many Orthodox leaders would no doubt wish to distance themselves from such statements and adopt a more positive attitude to the rights of non-Jews in the Land. Similarly, as we have seen, some take an extremely hawkish, others a much more dovish, view on the question of territorial concessions for the sake of peace. The latter, in addition to those already mentioned, include Rabbi Yehudah Amital, Professor Aviezer Ravitzky, Uriel Simon, David Kretchmer, and the late Professor Yeshayahu Leibowitz. Also needing to be acknowledged are Orthodox organizations such as *Oz v'Shalom* and *Netivei Shalom,* which have played an important role in supporting the Peace Now movement.

What is nevertheless striking about Orthodox Jewish *halakhic* literature on the subject—unless I am misled by insufficient acquaintance with it—is an astonishing lack of concern with, or emphasis upon, what seems to me so obviously the very nub of the problem: that the Land is the subject of conflicting claims by two peoples, Jewish and Palestinian, and that this conflict needs to be considered and settled in the light of universal-ethical principles.

In an otherwise ultra-Orthodox anthology, from which we have already quoted several times, one dissentient contributor, Yisrael Yaacov Yuval, writes:

> Action seen from a political-theological viewpoint as constituting a decisive stage in a divinely ordained redemptive process, appears to dispense with the need of applying moral criteria problems such as the subjugation of another people, the refugees and Arab claims to the country.... All types of nationalism are characterized by this kind of particularized mystique, that ignores the existence of generally valid rules of ethics.... It is against this startlingly simple theologico-political canvas, the natural outgrowth of Messianism where God demands acts of injustice towards one party in order to benefit his chosen favorite, that we find an explanation for an aristocratic ethic, so devoid of humanity.[38]

THE LIBERAL CONSCIENCE

A liberal view would begin by denying the whole fundamentalist basis on which the Orthodox view rests. It would say that the alleged divine promises contained in Scripture are not objective statements of God's Will but subjective perceptions of it that need to be understood in their historical context; that the fundamentalist reading of them rests on a misunderstanding of what the Bible is; and that the invocation of such texts to "prove" Jewish ownership of the Land three millennia later is altogether inadmissible.

Similarly, it would maintain that the concept of the "holiness" of the Land is only a matter of historical associations, not of supernatural reality, and has no relevance to the present debate. Likewise, it would contend that such issues as the borders of the Land and the rights of non-Jews within it need to be determined by considerations quite other than technical-legal interpretations of biblical and talmudic texts.

What these considerations are has already been indicated: they are universal-ethical considerations. That does not mean that they are extraneous to Judaism. On the contrary, they are very much rooted in Judaism, but in its general values rather than in its legal minutiae, and therefore in the teachings of the Prophets as well as the Torah, and of the *aggadah* as well as the *halakhah*. Although rooted in Judaism, these values also transcend it, because by their universal nature they rightfully claim, as they have in large measure received, the assent of civilized humanity. They are: justice, humaneness, compassion, democracy, the need for international law and order, and the imperative of peace.

Judged by these criteria, the Jewish claim to the Land is very strong and needs no support from an antiquated theology. The millennia-old association of the Jewish people with the Land; their persistent love and longing for it; their unjust expulsions from it (even though many emigrated of their own free will); the fact that they have nevertheless always maintained a presence in it; their desperate need for a haven of refuge from persecution, especially before and after the Holocaust; the agricultural achievements of the *chalutzim* (pioneers) who began to resettle the Land toward the end of the last century; the even greater cultural, economic, political, and military achievements of the State of Israel itself, including the absorption of a vast number of immigrants from Arab lands as well as from Ethiopia and the former Soviet Union: all these constitute an extremely powerful claim that no fair-minded person would deny.

But it is not an exclusive claim! The Land was not empty when the Zionist resettlement began. It had a large Arab population, which until after the Second World War still constituted a large majority. Many of these Arabs had lived in Palestine for many generations, even centuries, and were deeply attached to its soil. They understandably resented the ever-increasing Jewish immigration and, still more, the displacement of hundreds of thousands of their people during the War of Independence. They have therefore developed their own Palestinian nationalism, which is in many ways a mirror image of Jewish nationalism and demands similarly to be heard by the international community. Thus, the Palestinian-Arab claim to the Land, though different from the Jewish one, also has considerable weight.

That being the case, it has been totally obvious to liberal-minded people all along that if there is to be any kind of justice, the two peoples, Jewish and Arab, must in one way or another share the Land. One way might have been the creation of a binational state, as advocated by the first President of the Hebrew University, Judah L. Magnes, who was a Progressive rabbi; but that was rejected by both sides and left partition as the only remaining just option.

That has been the all but unanimous view of the international community for the past fifty years. It was the United Nations' partition resolution of 1947 that made possible the establishment of the State of Israel and gave it legitimacy in international law. Moreover, the partition principle has been periodically reaffirmed by the United Nations (for instance by Resolution 242 of 1967 and Resolution 338 of 1973), as it was affirmed yet again by the Preamble of the Camp David Accords of 1979, all of which the State of Israel has endorsed.

The current peace process, which began in 1991–92, honors the principle by calling for mutual recognition of Israel and the Palestinians and by promising the latter autonomy in Gaza and parts of the West Bank. The solution it envisages may be far from perfect and has yet to be fully worked out by negotiation, but it represents a large step toward a just solution of the conflict, or as just a solution as is now realistically attainable. As such, it should be welcomed and supported by all Jews both in Israel and in the Diaspora.

What is here argued is not a political but a religious view. It is predicated on the most basic principles of Judaism as Progressive Jews understand it: first, that the God of Judaism is the universal God, who has created all human beings in the Divine Image and cares for them with an impartial love, so that a prophet was able to say in God's name: "Blessed be Egypt My people, and Assyria the work of My hands, and Israel My heritage" (Isa. 19:25); second, that the God of Judaism is a moral God, so that justice and compassion are of the essence both of God's nature and of God's demands; for "the Eternal One is righteous, and loves righteous deeds" (Ps. 11:7); third, that God's plan for the future of humanity is a time when the nations will "beat their swords into plowshares, and their spears into pruning-hooks" (Isa. 2:4), and live together in amity, concord, and peace; fourth, that God expects the Jewish people, not only to pursue its own interest, but to set a moral example and so to be a "light unto the nations" (Isa. 49:6); and fifth, that this involves applying the principle of "[l]ove your neighbor" (Lev. 19:18) not only to interpersonal but also to international relations, so that we may not then deny to another people what we demand for ourselves.

It is these religious and moral principles that make it incumbent on Jews to seek a relationship of mutual respect, understanding, accommodation, and reconciliation with the Palestinian people. The present peace process gives Israel a unique opportunity to do that and so to demonstrate to a world crying out for just such a demonstration that it is possible to transcend nationalism, to show magnanimity, achieve compromise, and transform enmity into friendship.

The assassination of Yitzchak Rabin has tragically concentrated the minds of all Jews on the fateful choice Israel must make in the coming months. Our hope and prayer must be that the shock of it will renew and sustain the peace momentum until its goal has been attained, not only for reasons of realpolitik—that it is in Israel's own best interest—but for reasons grounded in the very essence of Jewish religion and ethics: because it is the will of the God of Judaism, who is the God of all humanity. To make that point again and again is the specific responsibility of Progressive Judaism.

JOHN D. RAYNER

Notes

1. See, for instance, Avner Tomaschoff, ed., *Whose Homeland, Eretz Yisrael, Roots of the Jewish Claim,* World Zionist Organization, Department for Torah Education and Culture in the Diaspora (Jerusalem: Achva Press, 5738 [1978]); J. David Bleich, *Contemporary Halakhic Problems* Vol. 2 (New York: Ktav, 1983), Chap. 8 on "The Sanctity of the Liberated Territories" and Chap. 9 on "Judea and Samaria: Settlement and Return"; Meyer Berlin and Shlomo Josef Zevin, eds., *Encyclopedia Talmudit* (Hebrew edition), Vol. 2, s.v. *Eretz Yisrael,* Fifth Printing (Jerusalem: Yad Harav Herzog [Emet] Press, 1979), pp. 199-235.

2. A rare exception is Moshe Zemer's *Halakhah Sh'fuyah* ("The Sane Halakhah") (Tel-Aviv: Dvir, 1993), especially Chap. 14b on *"Territories in Exchange for Peace."*

3. That statement does indeed require some important qualifications (see Shubert Spero, *Morality, Halakha and the Jewish Tradition* [New York: Ktav & Yeshivah University Press, 1983], especially Chap. 6), but I believe it holds true enough for our purposes.

4. Pes. 87b.

5. From the Concluding Service of the Day of Atonement, *Liberal Jewish Prayer Book,* Vol. 2, Ed. by Israel L. Mattuck, London: 1937, p. 281, based on David Einhorn's *Olat Tamid* of 1856.

6. *Kelim* 1:6.

7. Hyam Maccoby, "Does Halakhah Allow Surrender of Land?" in *The London Jewish Chronicle* 22 (October 1993).

8. *B.B.* 158a.

9. *Ket.* 110b.

10. *Ket.* 11a.

11. *Mechilta,* Pischa 1 to Exod. 12:1, Edited by Lauterbach, Vol. 1, p. 4.

12. *Chag.* 3b; *Mishneh Torah, Hilchot Terumot* 1:5; Bleich (see Note 1), pp.171-75; *Encyclopedia Talmudit* (see Note 1), pp. 113-16.

13. *Tosefta Shevi'it* 1:6; *Sifrei* Deut. 5.1 to Deut. 11:24; *Encyc. Talmudit,* pp. 116-18.

14. On the *halakhic* perspective, see sources in Note 1, especially Bleich and Yehudah Elizur, in *Whose Homeland,* pp. 42-53. On historical perspective, see *Encyc.Judaica,* Vol. 9, pp. 112-22.

15. Rav Yishai Yuval, in *Whose Homeland,* pp. 122f.

16. *Sifrei* Deut. 80 to Deut. 11:31f; *Tosefta AZ* 4(5):3.

THE LAND, THE LAW, AND THE LIBERAL CONSCIENCE

17. Rav Avraham Elkana-Shapira, in *Whose Land* (see Note 1), p. 166.

18. Nachmanides' Torah commentary to Num. 33:53 and his addendum No. 4 to Maimonides' *Sefer ha-Mitzvot, Mitzvot Aseh*.

19. *Encyclopedia Talmudit* (see Note 1), p. 223b. Maimonides does include the *mitzvah* in his Mishneh Torah, Hilchot Melachim 5:12.

20. Bleich (see Note 1), pp. 195f.

21. Ibid., p. 204.

22. Published by the Union of American Hebrew Congregations, 1981, pp. 1381f.

23. Bleich, op. cit., p. 211.

24. *AZ* 20a; *Mishneh Torah, Hilhot Avodat Kohavim* 10:3f, *Shulhan Arukh, Yoreh De'ah* 151:8.

25. *Mishneh Torah, Hilkhot Avodat Kohavim* 10:6.

26. Rav Yehoshuah Menachem Ehrenberg, in *Whose Homeland* (see Note 1), p. 178; cf. Maimonides, *Mishneh Torah, Hilkhot Melakhim* 8:10.

27. Ibid., p. 168.

28. Ibid., p. 170.

29. Ibid., p. 139.

30. Moshe Zemer (see Note 2), pp. 161ff, quoting *Torah she-b'al Peh*, ed. by Yitzchak Raphael (Jerusalem, 5740 [1980]), p. 14.

31. See Note 7.

32. *San.* 74a.

33. *Whose Homeland* (see Note 1), p. 115.

34. Ibid., p. 176.

35. Ibid., pp. 166ff.

36. Ibid., p. 96.

37. Ibid., p. 97.

38. Ibid., pp. 103, 104.

"THEY SHALL NOT MOUNT THE WALL FROM EXILE": THE "THREE OATHS" AS A BARRIER TO *ALIYAH* IN JEWISH HISTORY*

Aviezer Ravitsky

THE IDEA AND ITS IMPACT

The People of Israeli is scattered in every Land.... At the time that God shall remember our exile and lift up the horn of his Messiah, each one will say: "I will lead the Jews and I will gather them [in their Land]".... Were it not that we fear that the End has not yet come, we would gather together. But we cannot do so until the time of the song-bird is come and the voice of the turtledove is heard [in the Land], until the harbingers declare, "My God be great."[1]

This early document cited in the *Travels* of Benjamin of Tudela reflects the tensions generated by the question of the redemption and the Land of Israel among twelfth-century[2] German Jews—"mourners of Zion and mourners of Jerusalem."[3] These Jews, like many others before and since, are depicted here as vacillating between two opposing poles—the anticipation of imminent redemption and the traditional fear of forcing the End prematurely. For them, the Land of Israel and collective *aliyah* are explicitly messianic categories, an expression of their deepest religious longing, whose realization within history is forbidden,

---

* This is the last chapter of Professor Ravitzky's book, *Messianism, Zionism and Jewish Religious Radicalism,* University of Chicago Press, Chicago, 1996 (in print). We express our gratitude to the University of Chicago Press and to the author for their kind permission to publish this chapter. We have made some minor changes in punctuation and style to make this article consistent with the others in this volume.

"THEY SHALL NOT MOUNT THE WALL FROM EXILE"

"until there comes the time of the song-bird." These "mourners of Zion" are portrayed as speaking in all innocence, their words not representing an explicit ideological or theological position. Hence, the power that informs these words: "Were it not that we fear that the End has not yet come, we would gather together!"

The fear of mass *aliyah* to the Land of Israel was inherent in the oaths taken by the people of Israel—according to the Talmud and the midrashic literature—to accept the yoke of Exile, as well as in the primeval myth regarding the children of Ephraim who went up from Egypt prematurely and fell by the sword:

> What are these three oaths? One, that Israel not ascend the wall;[4] one, that the Holy One blessed be He adjured Israel not to rebel against the nations of the world; and one, that the Holy One blessed be He adjured the idolaters not to oppress Israel overly much *(BT Ketubot* 111a).

> For God said, [L]est the people regret when they see war [Exod. 13:17]. This is the war of the children of Ephraim... because they forced the End, and transgressed the oath *(Mehilta de-Rabbi Ishmae'el).*[5]

> R. Helbo said: "There are four oaths here: that they not rebel against the kingdoms; that they not force the End; that they not reveal their mystery to the nations of the world; and that they not ascend as a wall from the Exile." R. Onya said: "These four oaths correspond to the four generations which

forced the End and failed....[The children of Ephraim] gathered together and went to war, and many of them died. Why? Because they did not believe in God and did not trust His salvation, because they transgress the End and the oath." "Lest you awaken or excite my love" (Cant. R. 2.7).

These ideas assumed different garbs in the *midrashim* and the Aramaic to the Bible.[6] We do not know for certain the exact background that elicited these early warnings against collective breach. Our present concern, however, is with a different question: What impact would this concept have on Jewish sources and Jewish history? Was its imprint clear across the generations, from the Middle Ages into the modern period? Why has its influence grown in recent times?

Virtually all the students of religion and Zionism who have pondered these questions are in agreement. In their view, the concrete impact of the three oaths, both in literature and on the religious consciousness, has never been decisive; rather, these have always been treated as *aggadic* and nonbinding. Moreover, according to this view, throughout Jewish history the oaths never served as a direct barrier to *aliyah*. Their critical use, which was to emerge in the modern period, was almost exclusively the innovation of Western European proponents of emancipation and of Eastern European Orthodox opponents of Zionism.

I shall note here the words of two important scholars only. In 1979 Prof. Mordecai Breuer wrote:

"THEY SHALL NOT MOUNT THE WALL FROM EXILE"

Traditional Jewish thought understood the three oaths as landmarks for the people in Exile, not as proscriptions addressed against those who wished to go up to Zion. Hence, the oaths did not contradict the ascent of Jews to the Land of Israel, even in large and organized groups, so long as the Jewish dispersion remained in their exiles.... We have not found the three oaths explicitly cited as an ongoing halakhah.... Even with the organization of large and cohesive groups of immigrants, from the *aliyah* of R. Judah the Hasid, who came up [to the Land of Israel] at the head of a thousand Jews in 1700, through to the *aliyah* of Hasidim and disciples of the Gaon of Vilna—the question of the three oaths did not arise as a practical halakhic one.[7]

Ehud Luz, in his book *Parallels Meet,* summarized this question in a similar spirit:

It is in any case clear that in and of itself it could not provide a foundation for a *halakhic* prohibition.... Most of the pro-Emancipation Orthodox thinkers in Western Europe relied on this *midrash* to support their claim that no tangible efforts should be made to bring on the redemption before the days of the Messiah.... By contrast, it hardly appears in Eastern Europe before the advent of Herzlian Zionism.[8]

I, also, tended to support this view. A survey of the sources from both the Middle Ages and the modern period, however, has led me to reconsider this question. Close examination reveals that the wall placed by the oaths between the people and its land was far higher than historians suggest. It was a wall that sprang up over the generations, resting on two foundations:

First, the three oaths definitely served to create a certain distance and dissociation from the Land. They were repeatedly invoked, on various occasions, to deter possible mass *aliyah*. This was certainly the case when the attempt to emigrate to the Land was also connected with messianic fervor. It is true that this warning was more often voiced in the twentieth century than in the nineteenth, and in the nineteenth century more often than in the eighteenth; and in the modern period generally more than in the Middle Ages.

During the course of those long centuries, neither the Land of Israel nor "ascending the wall" from exile were concrete social options; the very fear of transgressing these oaths was repressed by the people of Israel. By contrast, when *aliyah* was perceived as a substantive possibility, and people stirred themselves to attempt the move, the warning was voiced anew. In a paradoxical manner, the appearance of the oaths serves as a kind of seismograph, measuring, as it were, the impact of the Land upon the life of the communities.

Secondly, the three oaths were cited by those Jewish sages who sought to develop a comprehensive metaphysical understanding of exilic existence. They were interwoven within those theoretical approaches that attributed deep theological meaning to Jewish life in the dispersion, endowing it with profound symbolic and mystical content. The two different uses of the oaths, of course, were mutually supportive.

In the following sections I shall attempt to elucidate these two elements and explore their foundation. To this end, I shall select specific sources that integrate the oaths in their context and treat them with reverence. Neglected by historical research, these sources now require renewed proof of their accumulated weight over time.[9]

FIRST IMPRINTS

The oaths first appear (after midrashic literature) in Hebrew poetical literature *(piyyut)*. Already in the sixth century C.E., Simeon ben Megas ha-Kohen referred to them in one of his *piyyutim:*

> From always and from antiquity / You who examine innards /
> With two oaths / You adjured the lion cubs /
> Saying: one, that they not force the future End /
> and one, not to rebel against the four kingdoms.[10]

More than four hundred years later, R. Samuel ben R. Hoshaya, one of the outstanding gaonic leaders of Palestine, composed a verse in the same spirit:

> I gave an oath to my multitudes not to rebel against the Wild One [Ishmael] and Edom
> Be silent, till the time that I make them as Sodom....
> I made you an oath, my careful ones, lest you rebel
> Await the End of Days and do not tremble.[11]

These *piyyutim* urge the people to accept the yoke of Exile and the Gentile world, but they do not deal directly with the question of *aliyah* to the Land of Israel. They offer no thematic innovations nor any particular historical context beyond the substance of the early *midrashim*.

During the entire period of the Muslim conquest (634-1099), *aliyah* was rare and of extremely limited scope. Scholars differ as to whether this should be attributed primarily to objective conditions—the economic distress and physical danger in Palestine during this period—or whether it was also connected with a certain rabbinic recoil regarding *aliyah* in pre-Messianic times.[12] In any event, it is clear that *aliyah* was not then perceived as religious-normative behavior, binding on the individual, and certainly not as a practical social option.

This is particularly striking in comparison with the repeated calls by the Karaite sages, who admonished their flocks to immigrate to the Land of Israel. In 900 C.E., the Karaite Daniel al-Qumisi severely condemned the ideaolgy of passivity toward the Land: "The scoundrels among the people of Israel say to one another: 'We need not go up to Jerusalem until we are ingathered by He who has thrust us out.' These are the words of the fools who provoked God's anger."[13] Al-Qumisi was perhaps protesting against a prevalent rabbinic approach of his time. Even if his remarks were directed solely toward the Karaites, the absence of a parallel call for *aliyah* by rabbinic leadership appears to be no accident.[14]

In other words, one should expect to hear the warning voice of the oaths precisely when *aliyah* out of the Exile "as a wall" was a concrete possibility and should not look for recognizable traces of the oaths in the contemporary literature.

Likewise, during the twelfth century, although a number of well-known rabbinic sages made pilgrimages to the Land of Israel, individual *aliyah* had not yet become an established form of behavior, let alone collective immigration and settlement. As mentioned above, a document attributing to German Jews an explicit fear of forcing the End by gathering in Zion is quoted in Rabbi Benjamin of Tudela's *Travels*. True, the source and date of this document are not entirely clear, nor is it certain that it was in fact written by R. Benjamin himself. Still, this document clearly exemplifies the reluctance regarding any attempt to actuate the messianic era within history.

Maimonides was probably the first rabbinic figure to adduce the oath as a warning against an actual social upheaval—in his admonition not to follow the imagined messiah who was then agitating the Jews of Yemen. Fearful of the political consequences and persecutions that might befall this community owing to the messianic turmoil, Maimonides tried to dissuade them from this path by every possible means. He wrote the following in the *Epistle to Yemen* (1172):

> Solomon of blessed memory, inspired by the Holy Spirit, foresaw that the prolonged duration of the exile would incite some of our people to seek to terminate it before the appointed time, and as a consequence they would perish or meet with disaster. Therefore he admonished them and adjured them in metaphorical language to desist, as we read: "I

adjure you, O maidens of Israel, by the gazelles or the hinds of the field, do not wake or rouse love until it please" [Cant. 2:7]. Now, brethren and friends, abide by the oath, and stir not up love until it pleases. And may God, Who created the world with the attribute of mercy, grant us to behold the ingathering of the exiles to the portion of His inheritance.[15]

We cannot ascribe decisive importance to the appearance of this idea in the *Epistle to Yemen,* however, as in it Maimonides drew on every means at his disposal, even if purely rhetorical, to rescue a Jewish community.[16] There are grounds for suspecting that it was only because of these circumstances that he related in this manner to the oath in question. No trace of the oaths is found in Maimonides' *halakhic* works, and he had little truck with the interpretation of the *Song of Songs* as a historical allegory of the relationship between God and the people of Israel that underlies the midrash of the oaths (as may be seen both in his great *halakhic* work and in his philosophic writing).[17] It would therefore seem that Maimonides' reference to the oaths bore more of a political or contingent than a *halakhic* or theological character.

ALIYAH AND RECOIL

The thirteenth century saw an important change in the relation of Diaspora Jews to the Land of Israel. *Aliyah* gradually became a common pattern of behavior among the sages, particularly in Western lands.[18] Already at the beginning of the century, groups of Jews, primarily from the French schools of the Tosaphists, settled in Jerusalem and elsewhere in the land of Israel.[19] These immigrations, as has recently become clear, had a well-defined, strictly religious motivation: the longing to fulfill the commandments that were conditional on residence in the Land and thereby to attain religious perfection. In other words, because the Land of Israel enables one to live a richer and fuller religious life, allowing for broader Torah observance, the immigrant rabbi performed a pious deed and subjected himself to a multitude of religious precepts applicable only in the Land. His *aliyah* was promoted neither by a messianic agitation nor by a mystical longing for the Holy; it was, rather, a concrete, normative entry through the *halakhic* gates of the Land of Israel.

During this same period, however, one of the major figures of *Ashkenazic* pietism or Hasidism, Eliezer ben Moshe of Wurzburg (a nephew of Judah he-Hasid), issued one of the strongest warnings against *aliyah* in the history of Jewish literature. As he saw it, any attempt to break through and ascend to the Land prior to messianic times would involve a metaphysical danger and a gross profanation of the Land's sanctity. He likened the Land of Israel to Mount Sinai as it was at the very moment of Divine revelation—forbidden to approach or touch. Anyone who dared to break through put his very soul in danger! In his words:

> "You shall limit the people round about" [Exod. 19:12]: around Jerusalem and around the Land of Israel.
> "Take heed to yourselves, lest you go up into the mountain—for He has adjured Israel not to force the End and not go up to the Land prematurely."
> "Into the mountain"—this is the Land of Israel and the Temple Mount: "nor touch its edge"—that they not

approach the Mount to build the Temple there before its time. Another explanation: "nor touch its edge"—that they neither postpone the End nor force it. And this is: "to touch its edge *(katzehu)*"—the End *(ketz)*.
"Whoever touches the mountain shall surely die": whoever hastens to go up to the Land of Israel shall surely die.
"No hand shall touch it, for he shall be stoned": whoever hastens [to go there] shall not live; whoever goes up before the End, for while the Exile persists they shall not go free.
"And when the horn sounds long, they shall ascend the mountain—when shall the people of Israel leave the Exile to ascend to the Land of Israel? When the horn shall be blown long [at the time of redemption]." [20]

The way to the Land of Israel was thus blocked by an iron wall. The Exile represents the reality of history; the Land, the utopia of the End of Days. Any attempt to remove the barriers separating them would be self-destructive: "Whoever hastens shall not live!" The author not only lent compelling, binding power to the oath not to force the messianic realization; he also heightened the traditional religious reluctance to approach the holy precinct, casting the whole Land of Israel as a religious object, a transcendent and awesome entity.

As Israel Ta-Shma has already observed,[21] one may presume that these extreme statements were not uttered in a void; they addressed a specific situation—that is, the concrete drive toward *aliyah* that had been renewed in the nearby schools of northern France. In fact, the very opposition to *aliyah* of a leading *Ashkenazic Hasid* is hardly surprising. He presumably received the idea from his predecessors, one of whom even wrote that whoever

"THEY SHALL NOT MOUNT THE WALL FROM EXILE"

went to the Land of Israel at the present time would not only not expiate his sins but, on the contrary, he "further multiplies his transgression" by "neglecting his marital obligation to multiply, the study of Torah, and prayer."[23] Not until our own time, however, do we again encounter an admonition as fierce as that of R. Eliezer of Wurzburg. In any event, this episode manifests two polarized approaches toward the Land of Israel: one by the French sages who were drawn to the Land by bonds of *mitzvot* and *halakhah,* and the other by German pietists, who turned away from the land because of their messianic conceptions and their religious fear of breaching the Holy.

ALIENATION OF THE *SHEKHINAH*

Only a few years later, R. Ezra, leader of the Kabbalist circle in Gerona, issued an appeal to the people to make their peace with the yoke of exile:

> At this time, the people of Israel are already exempted from the obligation of [living in] the Land of Israel. When they suffer Exile for the love of the Holy One blessed be He and undergo affliction for them: as it is said: "For Thy sake we are slain all the day" [Ps. 44:23].[23]

Thus, the concrete Land of Israel is not needed or required until the era of the Messiah: on the contrary, whoever goes there may be seen as forsaking the *Shekhinah,* which now dwells with the dispersed people of Israel.[24] R. Azriel, the disciple of R. Ezra (and apparently also his son-in-law) took a similar line.[25] He, too, set aside the Land of Israel during the pre-messianic period, asserting that the *Shekhinah* no longer dwelt there:

> Wherever the people of Israel went into Exile, sanctity dwells among them; therefore [the Holy One says], "I will not come to the city" which has been joined together, to the lower Jerusalem, until the time of the End, when Israel will return there; and [only then] the *Shekhinah* will return together with them.... During the time of the exile, however, because "the Holy One is in the midst of thee," He will not come to the city [Hos. 11:9].[26]

The idea of the exile of the *Shekhinah* illuminated the three oaths in a unique mystical light. The lower, historical exile reflects the metaphysical, supernal exile—the separation of the *Shekhinah* from its higher, divine source; the oaths disciplined the Jewish people to rebel against their Exile while the *Shekhinah* had not been delivered from its supernal exile. In the language of R. Ezra:

> "I have adjured thee": these are the words of the *Shekhinah* in the time of Exile; adjuring Israel not to force the End and not arouse Love until there comes the time of favor.... [At the present time, however], the *Shekhinah* is far from its place.[27]

As Haviva Pedaya noted,[28] R. Ezra may have connected the particular notion of the three oaths with specific Kabbalistic ideas regarding the concept of oath as such. According to this idea, the power of an oath forces itself upon the Godhead Itself. God, too, is bound by the vow until the End of Days. In any event, it is clear

"THEY SHALL NOT MOUNT THE WALL FROM EXILE"

that these oaths of passivity dovetailed with Ezra's mystical approach. Even at the time of redemption, he believed, the people of Israel will uphold their vow and not rebel against the nations of the world:

> Thereafter Israel, the scattered ones who are dispersed among the nations, will place upon themselves one head, that is, Messiah son of David who was with them in exile, and will go up to the Land of Israel by the permission of the kings of the nations and with their help!

That is to say, the Third Temple, like the Second, will also be built only with the consent of the Gentiles.[29]

Is it mere chance that the best-known immigrant to the Land in the thirteenth century, Rabbi Moses Nahmanides, emerged from this same circle of mystics in Gerona but profoundly disagreed with them as to the mystical status of the Land of Israel? Nahmanides took a diametrically opposed position on all the above questions. In contrast to the view exempting contemporary Jews from the obligation of living in the Land of Israel, Nahmanides was the first to formally establish the act of dwelling in the Land as "a positive commandment incumbent upon any individual in every generation, even in the time of Exile."[30] In contrast to R. Ezra's insistence that even in the messianic age the people of Israel will settle their land with the permission of other nations, Nahmanides insisted that "we not leave it [the Land] in the hands of other nations, *in any generation* [italics mine]."[31] Moreover, as opposed to the view distancing the *Shekhinah* from the Land until the messianic End, Nahmanides ascribed a supreme, exclusive significance to the religious life in the Holy Land. In fact, he denied any independent, inherent value to observing the commandments in the lands of Exile.³² No one before him had gone so far in placing the Land of Israel at the very center of Jewish teaching— not only in the age of the Messiah, but even in present historical time.³³

Does this ideological polarization between the passive position of Ezra and Azriel, who would defer *aliyah* to the messianic era, and the activist stance of Nahmanides indicate the existence of a dialogue and confrontation over this subject among the Gerona Kabbalists? It is not impossible. The young Nahmanides apparently learned Kabbalah from the elderly Ezra, whereas the latter used a work by the youthful Nahmanides.³⁴ By the time R. Ezra, in his last years, had set down his thoughts regarding the oaths and the permission of the nations, Nahmanides was already in his forties. We do not know, of course, the formative wellspring of Nahmanides' doctrine of the Land of Israel. Nevertheless, we may presume that the passive posture Ezra and Azriel adopted on this question was not divorced from the living presence of the Land in the consciousness of others, nor from the growing tendency toward *aliyah* in their own generation.

"THAT THEY NOT GO ON *ALIYAH* IN MULTITUDES"³⁵

Beginning with the fourteenth century our assumption that a dialectical relationship existed between the references to oaths and the phenomena of *aliyah* is no longer based upon circumstantial evidence alone. It has a clear basis in fact. Indeed, during this period, the edict of the oaths, which had originated in midrash and in Jewish thought, found its direct way into *halakhic* literature too. Apparently, only after Nahmanides' ruling that made dwelling in the Land an obligatory precept for future generations, and only when this ruling became widely known, was there a counter-reaction, in which the three oaths were powerfully reinvoked and even worked into the realm of *halakhic* discussion.

Interestingly, this reaction is first apparent in the writings of those very sages who felt drawn to the Land of Israel but considered themselves obligated by the oaths to qualify their positive attitude toward *aliyah*. They therefore distinguished clearly between the piously motivated move of an individual to the Land, which was blessed, and a collective break out of Exile, which was forbidden.

Thus, Estori ha-Parhi, an aficianado of the Land of Israel and a researcher of its antiquities, cited a Talmudic saying praising those who dwell in the Land, yet hedged it with restrictions and denied any Jewish longing to acquire political control there in the present age:

> [We read] in the Jerusalem Talmud, *Shekalim* (3:4): "It was taught in the name of Rabbi Meir: Whoever dwells permanently in the Land of Israel and speaks the Holy Tongue, etc., is assured his share in the World to Come." However, they may not go up in order to conquer until the End comes as is stated at the end of tractate *Ketubot:* "'Lest you arouse and awaken [the love]'... they should not ascend the wall."[36]

This restriction was formulated in the Land of Israel itself at the beginning of the fourteenth century. Indeed, its author saw fit to characterize his own personal *aliyah* in the same spirit: "[God] who knows every secret, knows that our [only] intention is to become sanctified by the holiness of the soil of Israel. We go there in awe [*eimah*], not to ascend the wall [*homah*]!"[37] Estori ha-Parhi may have been responding here directly to contemporary opposition to *aliyah*.

At the end of the century we find similar restrictions in a *halakhic* responsum written in North Africa by Isaac bar Sheshet (Ribash). This sage, a refugee of the persecutions of 1391 in Spain, ruled on the question of *aliyah* in accordance with Nahmanides: "*Aliyah* to the Land of Israel is a *mitzvah.*" Surely, this dictum reflected the situation of Spanish Jewry following the pogroms, which inspired the move to the Land. At the same time, the writer warned against any attempt to make a mass break from the exile:

> The prophet said to the people—"Build yourself houses" [Jer. 29:5]—addressing himself to those living in the Exile decreed upon them...: Now, too, one of the three oaths the Holy One blessed be He made Israel take is not to ascend the wall.[38]

Similarly, Solomon b. Simeon Duran (Rashbash) of Algiers, a son of a refugee from those same pogroms, was asked a concrete *halakhic* question pertaining to *aliyah*. He responded in like spirit, taking great care to eliminate any possible messianic connotation accruing to *aliyah:* "It is incumbent upon every individual to go up to live in the Land of Israel." He wrote:

> However, this is not an all-inclusive commandment for the entire people of Israel in their Exile but is withheld from the collectivity[39].... For one of the

"THEY SHALL NOT MOUNT THE WALL FROM EXILE"

oaths the Holy One blessed be He adjured Israel was not to hasten the End and not to ascend the wall. Consider what happened to the children of Ephraim when they forced the End prematurely.[40]

Just as the opponent of *aliyah* made the Land of Israel a strictly messianic category, the proponents of *aliyah* attempted to dissociate the Land from any messianic context. To go to the Land, the latter said, is in fact an ongoing, binding commandment, but those who obey it are expected to be doubly careful to observe the high barriers separating the age of Exile from that of Redemption. They may not go up "in order to conquer" (Estori ha-Parhi); they may not "ascend the wall" against the will of the ruling peoples (Ribash); and they may not go up collectively—"the entire people" (Rashbash).[41]

During the second half of the fifteenth century, there occurred a mass movement in Castile—men, women and children—who travelled by sea to the Land of Israel. This type of awakening, unprecedented for generations, was probably connected with messianic fervor[42] and, as might be expected, aroused anger and suspicion among other contemporary Jews. The heads of the Jewish community in Saragossa were severely critical, emphasizing in a letter to their Castilian counterparts the dangers involved in a mass voyage to the Holy Land. In this protest it is difficult to separate theological considerations from pragmatic apprehensions of the Gentiles' reaction to such a move. In any event, this mass migration to the Land of Israel was openly denounced as an attempt to force the End and to meddle with messianic redemption. As the Castilians protested in their letter:

People of small value and great number have set out for the Land of Israel.... We do not know what gave rise to this great foolishness.... And if one will say: "[I]s it not well known and renowned from days of old that the people have always gone from every corner to the Land of Israel?" [we answer], "This is true, but they have done it only in small numbers each time, and with adequate privilege from the rulers of the lands; never has such a great crowd been reported to go there together.... Therefore, our learned brothers and leaders, we beseech you: Let all those making this move turn back, let every person return home in peace, lest this hasten the End as the children of Ephraim did, heaven forfend.... [We pray that] our eyes shall see the Lord returning to Zion...and all of the people of Israel shall [follow] and ascend there to see the presence of the Lord our God in His chosen house." [43]

Again, the oaths and their invocation thrust before us the way in which *aliyah* became an actual religious question in different eras and in different places. Their articulation in literature may reveal, paradoxically, the immediate presence of the Land of Israel in Jewish consciousness and its concrete impact upon the life of the communities. Although the three oaths were generally on the margins of Jewish discourse, from time to time they were drawn inside to build a high barrier between the people and the Land.

Two questions remain to be dealt with in this context: First, was the edict of the oaths in fact limited to the Jewish collectivity only, to mass *aliyah,* or did it sometimes stand in the way of individual Jews too?[44] As we have seen, already in the thirteenth century one can find some rabbinical reservations concerning *aliyah* as such—whether by individuals or by a group—rendering it an explicitly messianic category. The sixteenth century saw an additional *halakhic* (!) attempt in this direction, based explicitly upon the old message of the oaths. The author was R. Joseph de Leon, a Spanish immigrant in Italy. In his *halakhic* work, *Megillat Esther* (on Maimonides' *Sefer ha-Mitzvot),* de Leon sought to exempt even individual Jews from the call of the Land:

> The commandment to inherit the Land and dwell therein is not observed save in the days of Moses, Joshua, and David, and so long as the people of Israel have not been exiled from their land. After they were exiled, however, this commandment is not binding upon subsequent generations until the advent of the Messiah. On the contrary, we are commanded, according to the end of tractate *Ketubot,* not to rebel against the nations by conquering the Land...not to ascend the wall. As for Nahmanides' statement that the sages conceived the conquest of the Land to be an obligatory war, this statement refers to a future time, when we shall not be subjugated to the nations. But with regard to his [Nahmanides'] statement that the sage engaged in hyperbole in praising the act of dwelling in the Land, this refers specifically to the time when the Temple stands: now, however, there is no commandment to live there.[45]

The question of the Exile and the Land is not discussed here in terms of place, but of time; not with regard to geographical space, but to historical reality—both political and religious. In the absence of Jewish political sovereignty and without the Temple, the Land of Israel is, so to speak, beggared. It loses its power to bind and attract contemporary Jews. De Leon in this reinterpreted Nahmanides' ruling, which made dwelling in the Land a positive commandment binding upon all generations. Even if one does not read his comments as a response to an immediate concrete question of *aliyah*, one does find in them a principled *halakhic* attempt to cope with the claims of the Land.

Secondly, was the prohibition against "going up en masse" always connected with the apprehension of provoking the Gentiles and of rebelling against world kingdoms? Not necessarily. For example, R. Samuel Yaffe, *Ashkenazic* rabbi of the community of Constantinople at the end of the sixteenth century, stated that even if the ruling nations themselves were to consent to the ingathering of the Jewish exiles en masse, this would still not free the people from the constraint of the oaths. As Yaffe wrote in his commentary to the Song of Songs:

> "They should not ascend the wall" until they are redeemed by the Messiah.... It seems to me that this prohibition applies even with the permission of the [Gentile] kingdoms. As God has scattered us to the corners of the world, we have no right to be gathered together "as a wall" to the Land of Israel until God by His Messiah shall gather us.... "[T]hey shall not force the end" to be redeemed with a strong hand.[46]

"THEY SHALL NOT MOUNT THE WALL FROM EXILE"

Yaffe clearly ruled out any possibility of a Jewish return to Zion by natural means without a prophetic, miraculous revelation. Neither the historic-political reality nor the reaction of the Gentile nations is theologically relevant. We shall see later how R. Jonathan Eibuschutz further elaborated and refined this idea.

EXILE AND ITS MEANING

Many of the examples cited in the previous section reflected the predominant moods among Spanish Jewry and its refugees during a period of decline and displacement. Yet, in the wake of the expulsion from Spain and Portugal, which threatened to undermine the very Jewish exilic existence, a growing tendency emerged among Jewish thinkers to reflect upon Jewish history and destiny and to seek its metaphysical meaning. No wonder, then, that in this context, too, the three oaths found their organic place.

I will begin with a radical expression of this tendency. A major sixteenth-century Kabbalist in Safed, R. Abraham Galante, adduced a striking myth concerning the Portuguese *conversos* and their stubborn allegiance to the oaths. The passage in question appears in Galante's mystical commentary to the Ethics of the Fathers, *Zekhut Avot*.[47] The printed version of this passage, however, is confused and marred by lacunae (due to censorship?) and does not reflect its original force. I shall therefore cite the authentic text, as it has survived in manuscript form (Paris 866).

Galante offered a Kabbalistic interpretation to the words of the Mishnah: "Love work and hate rulership, and do not make yourself known to the authorities":

The *Shekhinah* was called "work" *(melakhah)* because now, in the secret of Exile, it is sentenced to labor, to give its overflow to the "external ones" [the evil forces] and to the seventy [heavenly] princes [of the Gentiles]. Lilith is called "rulership" *(rabbanut),* because she is now in rule. Go and see how many circuses and theaters are yet standing while the lodging place of our God lies in waste. [Nevertheless,] the whole struggle [with the powers of evil] is to be performed by prayer and petition only, that is to take place between you and your Creator alone. But "do not make yourself known to the authorities" *(rashut);* that is, do not take oaths against the [ruling] nations—do not rebel or wage war against them. [Indeed,] such a desire rose up in the hearts of the Jews of Portugal, who were all forced to convert. Realizing that they were twice as numerous as the Gentiles [around them], so they desired to lift up their heads, to kill [their persecutors] and seize the kingship. However, there was an elder one there who inquired concerning this, by means of the Tetragrammaton, and he was answered [from Heaven]: "Lest you arouse and awaken the love [prematurely]...." As our rabbis interpreted it: "The Holy One blessed be He adjured three oaths to Israel, one, that they should not rebel against him [*sic!*]."

In other words: the *converso* Jews, by virtue both of their numbers and of their magical power, should have been able to overcome their persecuters and "seize the kingship." During the time of

Exile, however, the political rule of the nations is paralleled by the metaphysical rule of evil. It is the edict of the Almighty, then, that during this era "kingship" (in both senses) would be in bondage to these foreign powers. Hence, any attempt to break through by physical strength or by magical power, thereby upsetting the political and cosmic order of Exile, is tantamount to open rebellion against the Godhead. The *conversos* therefore look upon themselves not to attempt such a breach and to remain loyal to the oath even at the price of submission and apostasy!

A sweeping cosmic and mythical burden is thus conferred on the oaths, well beyond their original mundane confines. They not only represent the passive acceptance of the historical exile and political subjugation of the people, but also imply a reconciliation with the cosmic exile and a metaphysical captivity of the *Shekhinah*.[48] In fact, Galante presented a striking antithesis to the famous story of Joseph de la Reina. In contrast to de la Reina's unseemly attempt to trap Satan by magical means and to bring about redemption prematurely,[49] the Portuguese *conversos* overcame such a temptation. They accepted exile and subjugation, upholding the divine oath. Thus, the proscription of the oaths is directed simultaneously against both physical and mystical activity. It carries still greater force even than forced religious conversion.

We turn now to a more central intellectual development of the sixteenth century, one which would have a profound impact upon later generations. This was the doctrine of exile developed by Judah Loeb (Maharal) of Prague and the special role it ascribes to the decree of the oaths. The Maharal considered the phenomenon of exile less from the point of view of Jewish subjugation (like Galante) than from that of Jewish alienation.[50] Exile, of course, is a historical situation of a nation driven from its organic home and banished into an estranged existence among the Gentiles. At a deeper level, however, the nation's historical exile represents its metaphysical, existential estrangement to the very nature of the temporal world. Israel, the chosen people, has transcended the given, unredeemed order of reality. It belongs to a different order that has not yet coalesced and is consequently fated to experience the present time in an unnatural, exilic existence. The people of Israel is out of place and time—in every place and time—

> for the portion of Jacob is the portion of the world to come.... The people of Israel are persecuted, oppressed and harassed in this world, because this world is not worthy of them; hence, they confront opposition in this world.[51]

Exile is indeed a divine decree. But it does not so much stem from Israel's sin and punishment as reflect its innate essence. The Exile is indeed an anomaly,[52] yet in an unredeemed world this anomaly itself is the norm for the chosen people. As might be expected, the three oaths dovetail with this idea: they decree that the people of Israel will continue to experience an alien existence, and they call upon them to deviate from the natural order of space and time. At the same time, they produce a kind of "balanced" status quo between Israel and the nations. Israel will be submissive and not rebel, while the nations will allow the Jews to exist under their rule and will not oppress them to excess. The oaths, then, bring into being a unique social order:

> Exile represents a change in the order of the world. Such a change of order is difficult to sustain: there

is always a desire to negate it "that is, to gather together out of exile and ascend the wall.... God, therefore, decreed that Israel is not to rebel against the nations by leaving their rule ... and that the nations not subjugate Israel overly much, for otherwise the Exile could not exist.... He decreed that [the people] not ascend the wall and ingather the Exiles ... that they not force the End [even] by means of prayer and petition[53].... He adjured them by heaven and earth: just as the latters keep the [cosmic] law ordained by God with no alteration, thus Israel will keep that which God, may He be blessed, has decreed upon [it] in...Exile.[54]

In sum, the three oaths reflect the metahistorical nature of the Jewish people. Indeed, the Maharal took the oaths to an extreme: he demanded that persecuted Jews sacrifice their lives rather than uproot the Exile: "Even if [the Gentiles] shall wish to kill them with harsh tortures, Israel should not leave Exile and not alter this order!"[55]

The Maharal's central position in the history of Jewish thought led scholars and ideologues of the last generation— Zionists and anti-Zionists alike—to reinterpret his works according to their own contemporary conceptions. Some, such as Rabbi M. M. Kasher,[56] sought to minimize the force of oaths. According to this interpretation, the Maharal understood the oaths as a supernal decree imposed upon historical reality, rather than as a normative demand placed upon man. The oaths were intended to define the objective situation in the time of Exile, rather than to place restrictions upon the Jewish people. Such a reading of the Maharal, however, is incompatible with the overall context of his ideas. The Maharal dealt explicitly with both demands upon man and the divine decree upon reality. As he wrote in *Re'er ha-Golah:*

> The sages warned us to accept the dominion of the nations....[T]his proscription not to rebel against the nations' kingdom is so harsh, to the point that [if we break it] our flesh may be stripped away, Heaven forbid, like that of gazelles or hinds of the field [who fall prey].... Israel must not negate God's decree by force, but rather should pray for the return of the kingship of Israel.[57]

On the other hand, some interpretations of the Maharal take the opposite view, exaggerating the oath's prohibitions. According to the late Satmar Rebbe, Yoel Teitelbaum,[58] the Maharal stated, paradoxically, that even if the foreign nations should force the people of Israel to return to their land, they are commanded to resist such a "decree" with great devotion and treat it as though it were "an edict of apostasy." They are to prefer death to leaving the Exile! Against this claim, however, it seems clear that the Maharal is referring to the threat of death and "difficult tortures" stemming from the very conditions of life in Exile, rather than from expulsion from the Exile. Even so, his words are as hard as diamonds:

> If Israel abandon the divine decree of Exile it will be [its] destruction in Exile.... [Even so the people] endured cruel and harsh suffering...even if [the nations] should wish to kill them with tortures, they may leave [Exile].[59]

"THEY SHALL NOT MOUNT THE WALL FROM EXILE"

R. Isaiah Horowitz (Shelah), too, a great seventeenth-century sage, who himself settled in the land of Israel, tended to emphasize the metaphysical significance of the Exile in connection with the oath's decree. According to him, too, the mundane exile symbolizes the supernal exile; hence, one ought to be reconciled to its yoke:

> During the period of Exile, in which our great sins have engendered a separation within the supernal worlds, we must suffer, as stated in the Midrash, "I have adjured you" not to rebel. On the contrary, we are commanded to be submissive.[60]

Horowitz, I should emphasize, attached great importance to individual *aliyah* to the land of Exile, so that one might sanctify himself and fulfill the *mitzvot* that are [applied] there.[61] This act of individual ascent, however, occurs entirely in the age of Exile, of national political passivity. It does not bring release in any way from the prohibitions dictated by the historical pre-messianic realm. As Shelah wrote elsewhere:

> All of the [biblical] battles of Jacob with Esau allude to the [national] future.... Thus do we behave in our own generation, too, toward the children of Esau: our power is in our mouths only, that we may pray to God, may He be blessed, in times of trouble; but war, that is, fighting the nations [by the sword] does not pertain to us. Rather, we make "war" by the efforts of our community emissaries, who are obligated to show their faces to kings and princes to speak on behalf of Israel with all their strength....

> This is the pillar of Exile...until our righteous Messiah comes.[62]

This is here a clear echo of the fourteenth-century teachings of R. Banya ben Asher, who wrote:

> We should follow in the footsteps of our forefathers, that is, to prepare ourselves to approach the children of Esau with gifts, and with humble language, and with prayer to God, may He be blessed. It is impossible for us to meet them in war, as it is said, "I have adjured you, O daughters of Jerusalem" not to provoke war with the nations.[63]

This aspect of the oaths, prohibiting the people of Israel from waging war during the time of Exile, will resurface more strongly in later generations, beginning with the modern Hibbat Zion movement.[64] Horowitz understood Exile less as a punishment than as a moment in the continuing dialectic process of the sanctification of the nation. Exile is a necessary descent for the purpose of ascent:

> It is all for our good, that we may become refined in the furnace of the nations ... the light will come from the very darkness ... the curse itself will be turned into a blessing ... for destruction is the cause of true construction.[65]

In sum, during this age the Land of Israel would sanctify the righteous individuals, while Exile would purify the nation as a whole.

"THEY SHALL NOT MOUNT THE WALL FROM EXILE"

LANDMARKS IN THE MODERN PERIOD

We found the three oaths resonating during the Middle Ages into main, interconnected contexts: in relation to the practical question of *aliyah* and in relation to the theological question of Jewish existence in Exile. In the modern period the notion of the oaths arose in the same contexts. Indeed, they were invoked with particular frequency following the failure of the Sabbatean movement. I shall note several high points in the later development of the idea.

A. The most interesting treatment of the *midrash* of the oaths, following Horowitz, appears in the writings of the two great rivals—Jacob Emden and Jonathan Eibuhschuz—both sages eloquent in the praises of the Land of Israel.

Beginning with the second half of the seventeenth century, several large groups of European Jews attempted to settle in the Land of Israel. The most important of these, led by R. Judah he-Hasid,[66] came to the Land of Israel in 1700. The group was driven by messianic fervor, and its members were even suspected of harboring Sabbatean tendencies. R. Jacob Emden, for one who relentlessly persecuted every remnant of the Sabbatean movement, was severely critical of the group:

> There has sprung up a new sect of pietists in Poland, the fellowship of Judah he-Hasid, whose whole enterprise is built upon the fallen, vain foundation of Sabbatai Zevi, may the name of evildoers rot.... They did bizarre things; they promised to bring the

Messiah in a short time and went up as a wall[67] to the Land of Israel![68]

Emden himself was enthusiastic about *aliyah*. He imputed false messianic tendencies to this group, however, and accused them therefore of forcing the End and going up "as a wall."

Indeed, Emden ascribed considerable importance to the edict of the oaths, as a tocsin against false messianism. He even devoted a special prayer to it: "Master of the Universe, be Thou for us a God of salvation from the Exile; for You have adjured us with four oaths lest we ourselves do anything to force the End but only await [Your] salvation."[69] In fact, this strong-minded sage viewed the entire Sabbatean movement as a catastrophic transgression of the oaths. Emden perceived Sabbateanism as a demonic breach—an anti-messianic messianism, as it were—that stood as an obstacle to Israel's true redemption, causing the people to miss the hour of supreme grace (the same thing would be said years later by the Satmar Hasidim and the Neturei Karta concerning the Zionist movement). In Emden's words:

> One must know that in truth this event [of Sabbateanism] did not happen a natural way.... No doubt there was then a fortunate moment when redemption and salvation were imminent, had they not forced the End and violated the oaths.... The spirit of falsehood was permitted to mislead Israel and to confuse the world.[70] [Sabbatai Zevi] forced the hour; therefore the hour forced him and was turned to evil.[71]

Likewise, R. Moses Hagiz, Emden's stalwart colleague in the struggle against the vestiges of Sabbateanism, warned sharply about the punishment for forcing the End:

> For during that same period [of Sabbatai Zevi] the plague began. Nearly all the people of Israel were severely endangered; there was little between them and death, Heaven forbid, lest they would be judged as rebels and violators of the oath which God adjured Israel when they were exiled in the tents of Edom [Christianity] and Ishmael [Islam].[72]

In that period, then, the edict of the oaths clearly played a role similar to the one designated for it already in Maimonides' *Epistle to Yemen*. It was to stand in the breach against any false messianic agitation.

B. This is not the case in *Ahavat Yehonatan* by R. Jonathan Eibeschutz, which does not contain a strong warning against messianism but against *aliyah* en masse from the Exile.[73] Eibeschutz's doctrine of exile is a recondite, complex one that I have discussed at length elsewhere.[74] Suffice it to note that Eibeschutz conferred a definitive, radical interpretation on the edict of the oaths as only few sages—both before and after him—have done. As he put it:

> The congregation of Israel shouted out their vow— "Lest you arouse and awaken the love"—against the ingathering of Israel. For even if the whole people of Israel is prepared to go to Jerusalem, and even if all the nations consent, nevertheless, it is absolutely forbidden to go there. Because the End is unknown

and perhaps this is the wrong time.... [Indeed,] tomorrow or the next day they might sin, and will yet again need to go into Exile, Heaven forbid, and the latter [Exile] will be harsher than the former. Therefore the Congregation of Israel beseeched—"until it shall please"—that is to say: until the time comes when the entire world shall be filled with knowledge [of the Lord].[75]

The emphatic assertion that even the hypothetical support of the ruling nations to the ingathering of the exiles would not release Israel from the oaths is of particular interest. As we saw, R. Samuel Yafeh wrote in a similar vein at the end of the sixteenth century. But Eibeschutz went further, applying this assertion even to those who returned to the Land in biblical times from Babylonia to build the Second Jewish Commonwealth.[76] According to him, the call of the prophet Zechariah—"not by might, nor by power, but by my spirit"—as directed against the aspiration of these newcomers to ingather the entire exile "by force" before the messianic days.[78] That is to say, not even the declaration of Cyrus the Great overruled the prohibition on the people of Israel not to go up to the Land from the Exile en masse. Historical and political reality makes no difference to the basic theological norm. On the contrary, the latter remains valid in all non-messianic times, precluding collective *aliyah:* The Holy One blessed be He adjured the congregation of Israel not to go up before their Time."[79]

C. The notion of the oaths was later involved frequently in Hasidic literature.[80] The founders of Hasidism who neutralized the social-historical element of messianism in everyday religious life, referred to this notion both to warn of rebellion against the Exile by means of political activity and against forcing the End through spiritual-mystical efforts. On the one hand, R. Yaakov Yosef of Polonoyve (before 1780), taught the doctrine of political passivity: "The Holy One, blessed be He, adjured Israel neither to rebel against the nations nor leave the Exile until the Last Days."[81] On the other hand, R. Elimelekh of Lizhensk (1786), warned his followers not to overdo their mystical outbursts: "One should not exert oneself to exhaust them [the powers of impurity] completely and thereby cause the immediate coming of the Messiah, for our sages said: It is forbidden to force the End."[82] Warnings of this kind were repeated in dozens of homilies of Hasidic masters from the "Hozeh" of Lublin (R. Yaakov Yosef) and his disciples[83] in the early nineteenth century until the latter-day Hasidic opponents of Zionism. There is no room here to discuss the prolific Hasidic sources that invoked, over generations, the midrash of the oaths and the edict of Jewish passivity.[84]

D. Concurrently, the notion of the oaths played a leading role among the Orthodox seekers of Emancipation in Western Europe. It provided them religious grounds for opposing collective *aliyah* as well as any other political-historical initiative during the time of the Exile. As I have mentioned elsewhere, Moses Mendelssohn already declared that the Talmudic sages prohibited taking "the smallest step in the direction of forcing a return and a restoration of our nation."[85] At the beginning of the nineteenth century, the rabbi of the community of Emden, R. Abraham Lebenstamm, wrote in a similar vein. In his words, even if "we are capable of going up to Jerusalem by force of arms ... we are not permitted to take any initiative so as not to violate the divine oaths."[86] This theme was emphasized more firmly by R. Samson Raphael Hirsch, the leader of German Neo-Orthodoxy. Hirsch, indeed, injected a clear antipolitical slant into the oath "that they not ascend the wall," glossing it to mean that the children of Israel shall never seek to reestablish their nation by themselves (this in 1837!).[87] We find echoes of this approach in later generations as well.[88]

E. The message of the three oaths was also articulated in that period on the fringes of the well-known *aliyah* of the *Perushim* associated with the school of R. Elijah, the Gaon of Vilna. "Our sages indeed praise dwelling in the Land of Israel," wrote Zevi Hirsch Lehren in Amsterdam. "But until our Father in Heaven shall wish to redeem us, all buildings [in the Land] are vanity and emptiness." Lehren repeatedly called upon the dwellers in the Land of Israel to behave even there in accordance with the edict of Exile, in both the political and religious spheres. As for the political: "We are servants of the ruling kingdom. It does not become us, therefore, to be lifted above them until it please." As for the religious realm: one indeed ought to pray for the return of the *Shekhinah* from its exile, but "one should not make a commotion about this.... [T]hey should not multiply supplications to hasten the End."[89]

As Aryeh Morgenstern has shown, other sages in the Diaspora who opposed the activity of the *Perushim* also drew on the rhetoric of the oaths. R. Solomon Berliner, rabbi of the Ashkenazic community in London, who protested against the peculiar contacts of the *Perushim* with members of the London Missionary Society, used the language of the oaths against them.[90] Around the same time, R. Moshe Teitelbaum, a leading Hasidic rabbi in Hungary (author of *Yismah Mosheh),* expressed himself even more forthrightly. Teitelbaum explicitly blamed the act of *aliyah* for the Safed earthquake of 1837 and for other ill events in the Land: "[All these] should teach us that it is the will of God, may He be blessed, that we not go up to the Land of Israel by our own power, but wait until our righteous Messiah leads us there."[91] Similar warnings were also voiced elsewhere at that time.

Moreover, the *Perushim* themselves took the edict of the oaths very seriously. Consequently, they made an attempt to invalidate the edict with respect to their own time and their specific action.[92] Ironically, perhaps, it was R. Israel of Shklov, head of the *Perushim* in Safed, who gave a firm, *halakhically* binding status to the oath not to ascend the wall. In his *Pe'at ha-Shulhan,* which deals entirely with the laws concerning the Land of Israel, Shklov wrote: "Dwelling in the Land of Israel is equivalent to obeying the entire Torah. Yet it is not an all-inclusive commandment incumbent upon the entire people of Israel. In the time of Exile it is incumbent upon each individual only." The author stated explicitly that he qualified the commandment to dwell in the Land in order to explain the edict "not to ascend the wall"; for were it incumbent upon all Israel, then they would all be obligated to go up collectively.[93] In fact, a similar position had already been expressed by the Rashbash in the fifteenth century.[40] Yet only now, in the nineteenth century, was that position included *ab initio* in an authoritative *halakhic* codex.

But let there be there no mistake: even in earlier generations the edict of the oaths were never absent from *halakhic* discussions. For example, in his novellae on the Talmud *(Penei Yehoshu'a),* R. Joshua Heshel Falk took pains to delimit the permission granted to "every Jewish individual to ascend to the Land of Israel" on the condition that "they not go up together by force to build the walls of Jerusalem."[94] By the early eighteenth century, another distinguished scholar, R. Samuel Edels (Maharsha) also added his voice, claiming explicitly that the oaths "also apply at the present time."[95] It bears stressing however, that the three oaths typically reside in the ideological and theological realm, not within the formal *halakhic* one.[96] Even when the prohibition did enter *halakhic* literature, it reflected the religious consciousness, or even the religious anxiety, more than it did strictly legal considerations. Hence, the question I have raised here is not whether the edicts of the oaths "were explicitly considered everlasting *halakhah.*" My concern is with their real impact upon Jewish life and literature, including *halakhic* literature.

CONCLUSION

In light of all the above, is it not surprising that the deep-seated reluctance to rebel against the Exile or to force the End reemerged with renewed force in reaction to the appearance of the modern movement of Hibbat Zion and even more strongly to the Zionist enterprise and the establishment of the State of Israel? At its sharpest, of course, we find this reluctance in the ultra-Orthodox polemics against the national movement. But it is equally apparent in the consistent grappling with the notion of the oaths in the writings of the Orthodox supporters of the project of settling the Land: from the "Forerunners of Zionism" and the "Lovers of Zion" of the nineteenth century, down to later, contemporary authors.[97] To quote R. Simhah ha-Kohen of Dvinsk, many rabbis did not support (the settlement enterprise),

> [E]ven those who sympathized with it in their hearts and wished to reach fruition kept their peace, lest the enthusiasts would overdo, and because of their fear

of the three oaths which the daughters of Jerusalem were adjured. Now, however, Providence has caused an order to be issued at the gathering of the enlightened countries at San Remo that the Land of Israel shall be for the people of Israel. Thus, the fear of the oaths has gone.... It is therefore incumbent upon every person to help in the utmost of his ability to fulfill the commandment [of settling the Land].[98]

Indeed, the three oaths have not been at the crux of Jewish history, contrary to the claim of the radical religious opponents of Zionism. They were understood primarily as a theological guideline rather than as a formal *halakhic* proscription. Some sages went even further and downplayed the compelling force of the oaths. R. Hayyim Vital, for example, restricted the edict to a particular time frame: "The oath is valid for one thousand years only."[99] On the other hand, R. Pinhas Ha-Levi Horowitz (author of *Sefer Haflahah*) confined it to a specific place: the people were warned not to ascend the wall from Babylonia, in particular, "so as not to forsake the [special] holiness residing there."[100] Moreover, from the words of the Gaon of Vilna one might conclude that the oath prohibited only a particular clearly defined act: "They have been adjured not to go out by themselves to build the Temple, the supernal rose, until the advent of the Messiah."[101] The most extreme position was taken by R. Moses Haggiz, who protested against

> the opinion of several fools, whom I have heard saying that every city and each country in which Israel dwell is today holy soil like the cities of Israel and Judah...and supporting their ranting by quoting

our sages about the three oaths Israel was adjured by God.[102]

Paradoxically, though, this trenchant protest, from an eighteenth-century seeker of Zion, is itself a clear indication of how deeply rooted the oaths were in the consciousness of other, contemporary Jews, and hence the barrier they represented to their potential *aliyah*.[103]

Indeed, even today the traditional fear against rising up from Exile as a wall is not confined solely to extreme, outspoken religious groups. It flows in other channels as well, some of them hidden, making its impact upon several religious trends. Thus, any attempt, scholarly or ideological, to ignore it or to describe it as a recently created phenomenon, *ex nihilo,* will miss one of the deepest roots of the tense interaction between the Jewish religion and the modern enterprise of Jewish national renewal.

Notes

1. Benjamin of Tudela, *Travels.* Edited by Adler (London, 1907), p. 72.

2. Scholars are divided as to whether this document was written by R. Benjamin himself or whether it found its way into his book from elsewhere. See S. Schechter "Jewish Saints in Medieval Germany," *Studies in Judaism* (Philadelphia, Jewish Publication Society, 1945), 3rd series, pp. 6-8.

3. Thus the language of the document. Concerning the mourners of Zion in Franco-Germany, see Yaakov Gartner, "The Consciousness of the Mourners of Zion as a Factor in the Development of the Customs for Tisha be-Av" (in Hebrew). *Milet* 2 (1984): 204-207.

4. Rashi's comment: "'not to ascend' together by force." R. Jacob Emden and R. Samuel Strashun suggested the reading *ha-homah* ("as a wall"), based upon the language of the Talmud in *BT Yoma* 9b (cf. Cant. R. 8:11; the novellum of Yavetz and Rashash to *Ketubot* 111a in various editions of the Talmud). Salomon Buber suggests the reading *ba-homah,* based upon the text brought in his edition of *Midrash Tanhuma* (Vilna, 1885) *Devarim,* Chap. 4: "That they not go up as multitudes."

"THEY SHALL NOT MOUNT THE WALL FROM EXILE"

5. *Mehilta de-Rabbi Yishmael*, ed. by Horovitz-Rabin (Frankfort, 1931), *Masekhta de-Vayehi, Petihta*.

6. See, for example, *Tanhuma, Devarim*. Chap. 4; Targ. Ps.- Jon. to Exod. 13:17. For explanations and detailed sources, cf. Joseph Heinemann, *Aggadot ve-toldoteihen* (Jerusalem, 1979), pp. 137-47; Yaakov Blidstein, "The Exodus from Egypt of the Children of Ephraim: Further Discussion" (in Hebrew), *Mehkerei Yerushalayim be-Mahshevet Yisrael* 5 (1986): 12-13; Louis Ginzberg, *The Legends of the Jews*, Vol. 6 (Philadelphia: Jewish Publication Society, 1968) p. 2; David Berger, "Three Topological Themes in Early Jewish Messianism," *AJS Review* 10 (1985):141ff.

7. Mordecai Breuer, "The Discussion Concerning the Three Oaths in Recent Generations" (in Hebrew), *Geulah u-Medinah* (Jerusalem, 1979), pp. 49-57.

8. Ehud Luz, *Parallels Meet*, pp. 215-17. Cf. Yosef Salmon, *Dat ve-Tzionut* (Jerusalem, 1990), pp. 314-15.

9. During the last generation, extensive rabbinic literature regarding the question of the oaths has been written, primarily in response to the book *Va-Yoel Moshe*, by R. Yoel Teitelbaum, the late Rebbe of Satmar. See M. M. Kasher, *Ha-Tekufah ha-Gedolah* (Jerusalem, 1969), pp. 150, 174-78, 195-97, 221, 272-81; Shmu'el Hakohen Weingarten, *Hiishbati Etkhem* (Jerusalem, 1973); Shlomo Aviner, "Clarifications Regarding 'That They Not Ascend as a Wall'" (in Hebrew), *No'am* 20 (1980): 4-28; Hayyim Zimmerman, *Torah l'Israel* (in English) (Jerusalem, 1978), pp. 9-35; Meir Blumenfeld, "Concerning the Oath That They Not Ascend as a Wall" (in Hebrew), *Shanah be-Shanah* (Jerusalem, 1974), pp. 148-53; A.Y. Waldenberg, *Tzitz Eliezer*, Vol. 10 (Jerusalem, 1970), Sec. 1 (Completions); Yisrael Stipanski, "The Redemption from Egypt, The Redemption from Babylonia, and the Future Redemption" (in Hebrew). *Or ha-Mizrah* (1973), 200-225; S. P. Frank, *Toldot Ze'ev*, Pt. 2 (Jerusalem, 1964), Sec. 24. Cf. Z. Y. Kook, *Mi-tokh ha-Torah ha-Goelet* (Jerusalem, 1982), p. 190.

10. Joseph Yahalom, *Piyyutei Shimon ben Nagas* (Jerusalem, 1984), p. 241.

11. The *piyyut* is published in *Gihzei Schechter*. Pt. 2 (New York, 1928), pp. 65, 70.

12. See Moshe Gil, *Eretz Yisrael ba-Tekufah ha-Muslemit ha-Rishonah (634-1099)*, Vol. 1 (Tel Aviv, 1983), pp. 499-508; idem., "*Aliyah* and Pilgrimage During the Period of the First Muslim Conquest (634-1099)" (in Hebrew). *Cathedra* 8 (1978): 124-33; Avraham Grossman, "*Aliyah* to the Land of Israel During the Period of the First Muslim Conquest" (in Hebrew). *Cathedra* 8 (1978): 136-44. See also the reactions of Shmuel Safrai and Haggi Ben Shammai, ibid., pp. 134-35, 145.

13. See Jacob Mann, "An Early Karaite Text," *JQR* 92 (1922): 286.

14. *Iggerot ha-Rambam* (Jerusalem, 1960), p. 189. See the commentary of Ibn Ezra to Cant. 8:7: "Solomon Said in his Holy Spirit: I have adjured you that you are not to awaken until there comes the End."

15. English translation from Abraham Halkin & David Hartman, *Crisis and Leadership: Epistles of Maimonides* (Philadelphia-New York-Jerusalem, 1985) pp. 130-31.

16. Regarding the rhetorical nature of Maimonides' Epistle and its goals, see: Abraham S. Halkin's introduction to his edition of *Iggeret Teman* (New York, 1952). pp. 27-30: Aviezer Ravitzky, *Al Da'at ha-Makom* (Jerusalem, 1991), p. 54, n. 52; [Halkin & Hartman, *Crisis and Leadership*, pp. 150-200].

17. In both these works, the Song of Songs is interpreted as a metaphysical allegory of the relationship between man and God (or the Active Intellect). See Joseph B. Soloveitchik, *"U-Viqashtem mi-sham," Ish ha-Halakhah; Galuy ve-nistar* (Jerusalem, 1979), pp. 119-20; Joseph Kapah, *Kovetz Ketavim*, Vol. 2 (Jerusalem, 1989). pp. 619-20; Ravitzky, ibid.

18. Elhanan Reiner, *"Aliyah* and Pilgrimage to the Land of Israel" (in Hebrew), Doctoral Dissertation, Hebrew University, Jerusalem, 1988, pp. 39-118.

19. Ephraim Kanarfogel, "The *Aliyah* of 'Three Hundred Rabbis' in 1211: Tosafist Attitudes Towards Settling in the Land of Israel," *JQR* 76 (1986): 191-212.

20. MS. Bodleian Opp. 202, fol. 106b.

21. Israel Ta-Shma, "A Note Concerning the Attitude of the Early Ashkenazic Scholars to *Aliyah*" (in Hebrew), *Shalem* 6 (1992): 315-18.

22. Ta-Shma, "Matters of the Land of Israel" (in Hebrew), *Shalem* 1 (1974): 81-82.

23. Gershom Scholem, "A New Document Concerning the History of the Early Kabbalah" (in Hebrew), *Sefer Bialik [Knesset]*, (Tel Aviv, 1934), pp. 161-62; Moshe Idel, "The Land of Israel in Medieval Kabbalah," in L. A. Hoffman, ed., *The Land of Israel:* Jewish Perspectives (Bloomington, Ind.: University of Indiana Press, 1986), pp. 170-87.

24. Haviva Pedaya, "Land of Spirit and Real Land" (see Aviezer Ravitsky, Messianism, Zionism and Religious Radicalism (Chicago: University of Chicago Press, 1996), Chap. 2, n. 36), pp. 244-49.

25. Isaiah Tishby, *Hikrei Kabbalah u-sheluhoteha* (Jerusalem, 1982), pp. 3-10.

26. R. Azriel, *Perush ha-Aggadot,* I. Tishby, ed., (Jerusalem, 1945), pp. 29-30.

27. R. Ezra, *Perush Shir ha-Shirim* (attributed to Nahmanides), in H. D. Chavell, ed., *Kitvei ha-Ramban*, Vol. 2 (Jerusalem, 1964), p. 514.

28. Pedaya, "The Spiritual vs. the Concrete Land," n. 71; idem., "'Flaw' and 'Correction' in the Concept of the Godhead in the Teachings of Rabbi Isaac the Blind" (in Hebrew), 9 (1987): 212.

29. R. Ezra, *Perush Shir ha-Shirim*, op cit., p. 519.

"THEY SHALL NOT MOUNT THE WALL FROM EXILE"

30. Nahmanides, addenda to *Sefer ha-Mitzvot of Maimonides, Mitzvat Aseh* 4 (printed with Maimonides' *Sefer-ha-Mitzvot*, Vol. 2 [Jerusalem, 1959], p. 42).

31. Ibid.

32. See Ravitzky, " 'Set Yourself Markers for Zion: The Development of an Idea" (in Hebrew) *Eretz Yisrael be-hagut ha-Yehudit*, pp. 8–13 and the sources quoted there.

33. Nahmanides nevertheless wished to attribute the small numbers in the *aliyah* following Cyrus's proclamation to the fact that "they did not wish to press the End" (Chavell, *Kitvei Ramban*, Vol. 1, p. 274).

34. Tishby, *Hikrei Kabbalah u-sheluhoteha*, pp. 6–7. Idel and Pedaya have already noted the opposition between Rabbi Ezra and Nahmanides concerning the question of *aliyah*.

35. According to Buber's reading of *Midrash Tanhuma* (above, n. 4): that "they should not press the End and that when they ascend from Exile they not come en masse."

36. Estori [Isaac ben Moses] ha-Parhi, *Kaftor va-Ferah* (Jerusalem, 1897), p. 197.

37. Ibid., p. 2.

38. *Teshuvot ha-Ribash* (Constantinople, 1546), Sec. 101. Cf. Shaul Yisraeli, *Eretz Hemdah* (Jerusalem 1988), p. 17; Eliezer Bashan, "Does Military-Political Struggle for Redemption Suit the Jewish Tradition?" (in Hebrew), *Petahim* 32 (1975): 13–14.

39. Yisrael Stipanski suggested the reading: "It is withheld from the collectivity." See his book, *Eretz Yisrael be-Sifrut ha-Teshuvot*, Vol. 1 (Jerusalem, 1967), p. 133, n. 3.

40. In another responsum Rashbash opposed the philosophical-spiritualistic position that ignored the value of the Land of Israel (and of the earthly dimension generally) in religious life. Rashbash sought to average the insult to the concrete religious act.

41. Cf. the commentary of R. Levi Gersonides to the Song of Songs (Koenigsburg, 1860). In his view, the oath requires Israel to go toward redemption in the proper order, stage by stage.

42. See Z. Dinur, "The *Aliyah* Movement from Spain to the Land of Israel Following the Pogroms of 1391" (in Hebrew), *Zion* 32 (1967): 161–74. Joseph Hacker has shown that the date of this awakening is to be postponed to the second half of the century. See his paper "The Relation of Spanish Jews to the Land of Israel and Their *Aliyah* (in Hebrew), *Cathedra* 36 (1985): 20–28. Cf. E. E. Urbach, "*Aliyah* and Abandonment of the Land in Historical Perspective" (in Hebrew), in his *Al Tzionut ve-Yahadut: Iyyunim u-Masot* (Jerusalem, 1985), pp. 152–54.

43. Dinur, ibid.

44. At the end of the nineteenth century, R. Yeruham Perlman, the "Minsker Gadol," made unusual use of the idea of the oaths. According to him the edict was specifically intended to restrain the

yearning of many individuals to go up to the Land of Israel: "All of the commandments are incumbent personally and categorically.... Each Jewish individual is obligated to perform them without any conditions or limitation. The commandment of dwelling in the Land of Israel however is incumbent only upon the people as a whole. The rabbis anticipated in their holy spirit that if this commandment would be imposed upon each individual, the people would break through any bounds and would flow to the Land by the thousands from the four corners of the earth.... Therefore our Rabbis informed us that the Holy One adjured Israel that they not ascend the wall and not rebel against the nations.... The power of the commandment is thus weakened...because of the need of the hour" (see *Sinai* 6 [1940]: 210-21).

45. Isaac de Leon, *Megillat Esther* on Maimonides' *Sefer ha-Mitzvot, Mitzvat Aseh* 4 (ed. Jerusalem, 1959, Pt. 2, p. 42).

46. Shmuel Yaffe, *Yefeh Kol* (Izmir, 1739), fol. 71a. The primeval myth of the children of Ephraim, who went up from Egypt prematurely, served Yaffe as an archetype for the dangers of forcing the End: "They thought to go out by force.... [T]hey did not trust God, but their own sword and arm... [T]hey did not fear the oath not to arouse until God wishes it; thus they violated [the prohibition not to go before] the End."

47. Galante's interpretation is printed in the book *Bet Avot* (Belgrade, 1911), I, x; p. 91.

48. See *Sefer ha-Zohar* II:9a.

49. Compare the demand of the anonymous fifteenth-century Kabbalist to refrain from any mystical or magical activity to hasten the redemption *(Perush le-Shir ha-Shirim,* MS. Schocken—Kabbalah 10, fol. 42a). Moshe Idel observed that this Kabbalist rejected the activist-messianic approach of Kabbalists from the circle of *Sefer ha-Meshiv,* who attempted to overcome the powers of evil by magical means. See Idel's introduction to A. Z. Escoly, *ha-Tenuah ha-Meshihit be-Yisrael* (Jerusalem, 1987), p. 19.

50. See Rivka Schatz, "Existence and Eschatology in the Teachings of the Maharal," *Immanuel* 14 (1982): 86-97; 15 (1982-83): 62-72; Benjamin Gross, *Netzah Yisrael* (Jerusalem - Tel Aviv, 1974), pp. 128-69; Shalom Rosenberg, "Exile and Redemption in Jewish Thought in the Sixteenth Century: Contending Conceptions," in B. D. Cooperman, ed., *Jewish Thought in the Sixteenth Century* (Cambridge, Mass.: Harvard University Press, 1983), pp. 399-430; Andre Neher, *Le Puits de l'Exile* (Paris, 1966); B. L. Sherwin, *Mystical Theology and Social Dissent* (London and Toronto, 1982).

51. R. Judah Loeb of Prague, *Netzah Yisra'el* (Jerusalem, 1971), p. 89 (Chap. 16).

52. *Netzah Yisra'el,* p. 9 (Chap. l); p. 121 (Chap. 24). Cf. A. D. Kulka, "The Historical Background" (above, Chap. 2, n. 95), pp. 281-82.

53. See Rashi to *BT Ketubot* 111a. The prohibition against forcing the End by means of prayer was strongly emphasized in Hasidic literature. See also the remarks of R. Moshe Sofer (the Hatam Sofer) in *Eleh Divrei ha-Berit* (Altona, 1819), p. 42.

54. *Netzah Yisrael,* pp. 122-34 (Chap. 24).

"THEY SHALL NOT MOUNT THE WALL FROM EXILE"

55. *Netzah Yisrael*, p. 124.

56. *Ha-Tekufah ha-Gedolah*, pp. 272–81.

57. Maharal, *Be'er ha-Golah* (Jerusalem, 1971), p. 147 (Sec. 7).

58. Rabbi Yoel Teitelbaum, *Va-Yoel Moshe* (Jerusalem, 1978), *Ma'amar Shalosh Shevu'ot*, p. 38 (Sec. 20); p. 44 (Sec. 32); p. 91 (Sec. 76); p. 102 (Sec. 83); p. 103 (Sec. 86).

59. *Netzah Yisrael*

60. Isaiah Horowitz, Shenei Luhot ha-Berit, Pt. 3 (Warsaw, 19863; reported Jerusalem, 1963), p. 48b.

61. *Shenei Luhot ha-Berit*, Pt. 1, p. 56a; cf. 75b.

62. Ibid., Pt. 3, 24a. Cf. 49a, where the idea was directly connected to the subject of the oaths.

63. Bahye ben Asher, *Perush al ha-Torah* (Jerusalem, 1958), *Va-yishlah*, Gen. 32:7.

64. See below, n. 104.

65. *Shenei Luhot ha-Berit*, Pt. 2, 73a. Cf. ibid., 77a.

66. See Meir Benayahu, "The 'Holy Society' of Rabbi Judah he-Hasid" (in Hebrew), in *Sefer Yovel le-Shneur Zalman Shazar* (Jerusalem, 1960), pp. 133–82; Yaakov Barnai, *Yehudei Eretz-Yisrael ba-meah ha-Y"H* (Jerusalem, 1982), p. 28, and bibliography there.

67. See above, n. 4.

68. Yaakov Emden, *Torat ha-Kena'ot* (Amsterdam, 1752; Jerusalem, 1971), p. 48. See B. Z. Dinur, *Be-mifneh ha-dorot* (Jerusalem, 1972), p. 29.

69. Yaakov Emden, *Siddur Bet Ya'akov* (Warsaw, 1882), p. 80b.

70. *Torat ha-Kena'ot*, 2. See Liebes, "The Messianism of Emden" (above, Chap. 2, n. 66), p. 125.

71. *Torat ha-Kena'ot*, p. 132. In this spirit one should understand the emphasis placed by Emden upon the Talmudic aphorism that makes the removal of one's mind from messianic concerns a precondition for the coming of the Messiah (*BT Sanh.* 97b). See R. Yaakov Emden, *Hiddushim ve-Hagahot* on the Talmud (printed in standard editions of the Talmud), to *Ketubot* 111a.

72. Moshe Hagiz, *Shever Poshim* (Amsterdam, 1719), p. 6.

73. It was Emden, however, who condemned the massive *aliyah* of the circle of R. Yehudah ha-Hasid, also blaming R. Jonathan Eibuschutz for supporting this *aliyah*. See *Shevirat Luhot*

ha-Berit (Altona, 1756), p. 476a: "Several times he [Eibeschutz] spoke before them in praise of the suspect sect of R. Yehudah ha-Hasid, who had gone up to the Land of Israel."

74. See Ravitzky. " 'Set Yourself Markers,' " pp. 30-35.

75. Jonathan Eibuschutz, *Ahavat Yehonatan* (Warsaw, 1972), *Va-ethanan*, fol. 74a. Shmuel Weingarten, Hishbati etkhem, claims, in light of parallels in Eibuschutz's writings, that the national passivity is not presented here as a norm but as a fact, that it does not reflect a divine decree but the Jewish refusal to go up to the Land of Israel. Examination of these texts does not confirm his interpretation. On the contrary, God himself is portrayed by them as postponing the return of the people to Zion to days in which "the Evil Urge will be uprooted from the earth"—that is, to a metahistorical era.

76. Some Talmudic and Midrashic sayings condemn the Babylonian exiles for not ascending "as a wall" to the Second Commonwealth (see above, n. 4). This motif appears frequently in Jewish literature; Eibeschutz's opponent, R. Jacob Emden, likewise used it. Cf. above, n. 33; and Chap. 1, n. 67 (see n. 24).

77. Zech, 4:6.

78. *Ahavat Yehonatan, Miqez,* p. 19a.

79. Ibid., *Ki Teze,* p. 84a.; and cf. ibid., *Shoftim,* p. 82a.

80. Mendel Piekarcz cited a wealth of similar sources in his *Hasidut Polin* (Jerusalem, 1990). Cf. Yitzhak Alfasi, *Ha-Hasidut ve-Shivat Tzion* (Tel Aviv, 1986); Levi Yitzhak of Berdichev, *Kedushat Levi,* Pt. 1 (Jerusalem, 1964), pp. 103, 165; Shmuel Shemaryah of Strazov, *Zikhron Shemuel* (Warsaw, 1908), p. 13a.

81. Ya'akov Yosef of Polonoyye, *Toldot Ya'kov Yosef* (Koritz, 1780), p. 165c.

82. Elimelekh of Lizhensk, *Noam Elimelekh* (Levov, 1786), p. 54b. Cf. G. G. Scholem, "The Neutralization of the Messianic Element in Early Hasidism," *Journal of Jewish Studies* 44 (1969-70), p. 44; reprinted in his *The Messianic Idea in Judaism* (New York, 1971), pp. 176-202.

83. Yitzhak Ya'akov of Lublin, *Zikhron Zot* (Warsaw, 1869), p. 65d. Cf. the remarks of his disciple, R. Yaakov of Mialiscz, *Kol Ya'akov* (Jerusalem 1989), p. 361: "He may not give preference to the son of the beloved one [Deut. 21:16] that is, the congregation of Israel which is beloved to God 'before the son of the hated one,' so long as there continues the rule of the hated one. For our Creator has adjured us not to force the End."

84. I have not found the edict of the oaths directed against the Hasidic *aliyot* to the Land of Israel. See Israel Halperin, *Ha-Aliyot ha-Rishonot shel ha-Hasidim le-Eretz Yisrael* (Jerusalem-Tel Aviv, 1947); Yaakov Barnai, *Iggerot Hasidim mi-Eretz Yisrael* (Jerusalem, 1980); Hayyah Steinman-Katz, *Reshitan shel Aliyot Hasidim* (Jerusalem, 1987).

85. See above, n. 24.

"THEY SHALL NOT MOUNT THE WALL FROM EXILE"

86. Abraham Loewenstamm, *Tzeror ha-Hayyim* (Amsterdam, 1820), pp. 61-62.

87. S.R. Hirsch, *Horeb* (London - New York, 1962), Sec. 608, p. 461, discussion of three oaths.

88. See above n. 24. Only faint traces of this view appeared among Eastern Jewry. See, for example, in the words of R. Hayyim Palaggi, a great Sephardic sage in Turkey: the Holy One blessed be He adjured Israel that they not go up the wall... for God may He be blessed has scattered us to the four corners *(Otzrot ha-Hayyim* [Jerusalem, 1872] 37). But cf. his book *Nishmat Kol Hai* (Salonica 1832-37), *Yoreh Deah*, Sec. 49, 85; cf. Tubi, "The Roots of the Attitude" (above Chap. 2, n. 72), p. 182.

89. The sources appear in *Iggerot ha-Pekidim veha-Amarkalim me-Amsterdam* (MS Jerusalem - Ben-ZI Archives). Cf. Aryeh Morgenstern, Messianic Anticipations Preceding the Year 5600 (1840) (in Hebrew), in Z. Baras, ed., *Meshihiyut e-Eskhatologyah* (Jerusalem, 1984), pp. 351-52.

90. See idem., *Meshihiyut ve-Yishuv Eretz Yisrael* (Jerusalem, 1985), p. 107. Cf. ibid., pp. 25, 130, 182.

91. Moshe Teitelbaum, *Yismah Moshe*, Pyt. 1 (New York, 1947) end; cf. Alfasi, *Ha-Hasidut ve-Shivat Tzion*, p. 17.

92. Morgenstern, ibid., pp. 104-107.

93. Israel of Shklov, *Peat ha-Shulhan* (Jerusalem 1959), 1.3. Cf. in a letter of his: "The proscription of the oaths does not apply to individuals" Avraham Yaari, ed., *Iggerot Eretz Yisrael* (Tel Aviv, 1943), p. 355. Shklov also rejected the approach of R. Joseph De Leon *(Megillat Esther)*, cited above. See *Peat ha-Shulhan* 1.14.

94. Joshua Heshel Falk of Cracow, *Penei Yehoshu'a*, to BT Ket. 111a.

95. Shmuel Edels, *Hiddushei Halakhot va-Aggadot Maharsha*, in standard editions of the Talmud on *BT Ket.* 111a.

96. Cf. the remarks of R. Zeev Wolf Einhorn of Horodna (Maharzu) from the mid-nineteenth century in his commentary on Cant. R. 2:7: "King Messiah will bring all of Israel out of the Exile; if they do so by themselves, however, they will miss the messianic redemption." I wish to thank Dr. Hananel Mack for bringing this source to my attention.

97. See Kasher, *ha-Tekufah ha-Gedolah*, pp. 174-75. Cf. the letters in praise of settlement of the Land (from 1891) gathered in A. Y. Sluzki, *Shivat Tzion* (Warsaw 1900). The struggle with the edict of the oaths repeatedly appears as a motif in these letters: see ibid., Vol. 1, pp. 9, 35, 43, 51, 74; Vol. 2, pp. 16, 53, 84.

98. A letter of R. Meir Simhah ha-Kohen of Dvinsk from 1922. Cf. Simon Federbusch, *Torah u-Melukhah* (Jerusalem - New York, 1961), pp. 91-92.

99. Hayyim Vital, *Etz Hayyim* (Warsaw, 1931), Introduction.

100. Pinhas Halevi Horowitz, *Sefer ha-Hafla'ah*. Pt. I (Offenbach, 1787) on *BT Ket.* 111a.

101. *Siddur ha-Gera*, Pt. 2 (Jerusalem, 1891), p. 48a. For further sources, see Aviner Clarifications (above, n. 9).

102. Moshe Hagiz, *Sefat Emet* (Vilna, 1876; Jerusalem, 1968), p. 65.

103. Some rabbinical authorities have argued that from the moment the nations of the world violated their oath "not to oppress Israel overly much," Israel too is free of its oath. This view was raised in light of the 1929 Arab riots (see Y. M. Toledano, *Teshuvot Yam ha-Gadol* [Cairo, 1931], Sec. 97, p. 183) and, especially in light of the Holocaust, see Y. A. ha-Levi Herzog, "The Establishment of a State Prior to the Coming of the Messiah" (in Hebrew) *Sefer ha-Tzionut ha-Datit* (Jerusalem, 1977), p. 62. Some authorities have limited the prohibition of the oaths specifically to a military conquest of the Land. See Shmuel Mohilever, *Shivat Tzion*, Pt. I, p. 9; J. J. Reines, *Or Hadash al Tzion* (Vilna, 1902), 19b; Azriel Hildesheimer, *Gessammelte Aufsatze*, M. Hildesheimer, ed. (Frankfurt am Main, 1923), p. 216. Other rabbis have suggested a spiritualistic interpretation of the oaths, removing them entirely from the historical-political arena. See R. Abraham Burnstein of Sochaczew, *Avnei Nezer, Yoreh De'ah*, Sec. 456, p. 3: "The oath was directed to the root of their souls up above").

ALIYAH AND *YERIDAH* IN RABBINIC SOURCES

Judith Hauptman

Three decades ago, I lived in Israel for three years. Since then, I have lived in New York City. I was happy, therefore, to have the opportunity to examine rabbinic materials on the topic of *aliyah* and *yeridah*. Although I made my decision to leave Israel for personal reasons, independent of what ancient or modern Jewish texts have to say on the subject, I was still interested in discovering the views of the tradition on this matter.

Systematic investigation of rabbinic material has led me to realize that the different rabbinic works, such as the Mishnah, the Tosefta, the Babylonian Talmud, and the Jerusalem Talmud, all speak in different voices. The tendency for a long time has been to harmonize all these works and to assume that they all agree with each other, but this is not the case. I therefore think it worthwhile to see what each work on its own has to say on the topics of *aliyah* and *yeridah* and how those views compare with each other. The question I am asking is not what the codes ultimately decided, but what is the history and development of rabbinic thinking on this subject.

Instead of beginning with Mishnaic passages on *aliyah* and *yeridah,* I will first examine the relevant material in the Tosefta, the Mishnah's companion volume, dating from the same period. There is reason to believe that some Tosefta passages were composed at an earlier time than the parallel ones found in the Mishnah.

Talmud *Ketubot* 13:2 states:

> If he wishes to come to the Land of Israel but she does not, they force her to come. If she wishes to

come [to the Land of Israel] but he does not, they [do not] force him to come. If he wishes to leave the Land of Israel but she does not, they do not force her to leave. If she wishes [to leave] but he does not, they force her not to leave.

In some versions of the Tosefta, the second clause concludes with the statement that he *is* forced to move to Israel, but in others it says he is *not*.[1] That is, the two versions of the passage agree that a husband may force a wife to move to or remain in Israel but disagree about whether she may do the same to him. The probable reason for the existence of these two versions is that it was hard for some *tannaim,* and possibly even some copyists, over the course of time, to accept the idea that women could control men in this way.

If we read this Tosefta passage in context, we find that the larger issue is whether a husband may force a wife, upon marriage, to leave her parents' home in one part of Israel—for example, the Galilee—to move in with him in another part of Israel—for example, Judea. The answer is that he may determine, in general, the place where he and his wife will live, but certain restrictions apply.[2] The Tosefta then says that one may force a spouse to move from a primarily Gentile environment to a completely Jewish one but not from a primarily Jewish surrounding to a completely Gentile one.

After discussing these matters, the Tosefta, as noted above, speaks of forcing one's spouse to move to Israel.[3] What this paragraph teaches us is that although living outside of Israel is clearly sanctioned, living in Israel is strongly favored, to the extent that not only may he impose his will on her, but even she may impose hers on him. In this case a man may force a woman to move far away from her family. Similarly, if he wishes to leave Israel and she does not, he may not force her to leave. Her staying is privileged over his leaving. If living in Israel were an absolute obligation upon all Jews, this passage would not talk about moving to or leaving Israel only in the context of spouses in conflict, but would say something to the effect that all Jews should seek to make their home there. These statements imply that if neither spouse wishes to move to Israel, or if both wish to leave, it is perfectly all right for the couple to live outside of Israel.

If we now compare the Tosefta with the Mishnah, we find several noteworthy similarities and also differences. Like the Tosefta, Mishnah *Ketubot* 13:10 raises the issue of a husband forcing his wife to move, upon marriage, from one part of Israel to another. Mishnah 11 then says:

> All may force a spouse to move to Israel, but no one may force a spouse to leave. All may force a spouse to move to Jerusalem, but no one may force a spouse to leave. The same applies to men and to women (and to slaves).

Although this mishnah agrees with the Tosefta that one spouse may force another to move to or remain in Israel, its reformulation of the rule is rather striking. It says emphatically that either spouse may force the other to move to Israel, but neither spouse may force the other to leave, *and this holds true for men and women alike*. It is as if the author of this paragraph is saying in response to the Tosefta, which waffles, make no mistake about it, not only can men force women but even women can force men to move to or to stay in Israel. That is, the strong wording of this mishnah suggests that its author was aware of the fact that there was a Tannaitic dispute on this subject, some holding she could force him and some holding she could not, and that he comes to resolve it. Some versions of the Mishnah even allow a slave to force a master to move to or stay in Israel.[4]

All this notwithstanding, the Mishnah, like the Tosefta, is not saying there is an absolute obligation to live in Israel. If his wife does not force him to move there, he may continue to live in the *golah*. But if one spouse wishes to move to or remain in Israel, the other spouse must acquiesce. Since we would not go so far as to say that the second line of the Mishnah, which talks about moving to Jerusalem, obligates a Jew to live there, it follows that the first line, which talks about moving to Israel, similarly does not obligate a Jew to live there.

Both Talmuds, in commenting on this mishnah, cite the related Tosefta passage. The Babylonian Talmud version is especially noteworthy for the changes it has introduced. Babylonian Talmud *Ketubot* 110b:

> If he decides to go up [to Israel] and she decides not to, they force her to go. If not, she is divorced and forfeits the *ketubah* payment. If she decides to go up to Israel and he decides not to, they force him to go. If not, he divorces her and pays her the *ketubah* money. If she decides to leave ....

The first change in wording is that instead of saying, as does the Tosefta, to come to Israel, *lavo,* this *Baraita,* probably under the influence of the Mishnah, talks about going up to Israel, as we say today, "to make *aliyah.*" The second noticeable change, far more significant, is that the *Baraita* adds an escape clause to each of the four sections: he can move to Israel without forcing her to join him but may deprive her of the *ketubah* money; she can move to Israel without him and still collect her *ketubah* money; she can leave Israel without him but forfeit her *ketubah;* he can leave Israel without her but must still pay her the *ketubah.*[5]

All these clauses make the same point: no one can literally drag someone else to live in Israel, and no one can force someone else to stay in Israel. The financial penalties imposed on the spouse that does not wish to live there may push him or her to think the matter over again, but this is vastly different from saying that either spouse may force the other to move to or stay in Israel against the other's will. By altering the *Baraita* in this way, the Babylonian Talmud takes a step back from favoring living in Israel: not only is it not incumbent upon a Jew to live there, it is not even incumbent upon one spouse to live there if the other decides to move. Even so, the *Baraita* still favors living in Israel over keeping a marriage intact: another way of looking at it is that living in Israel is favored over keeping a marriage intact: better to live in Israel as a divorce(e) than in the *golah* married.[6]

It is only in the Babylonian Talmud, not in the Jerusalem Talmud version and not in the Tosefta original, that these additional words appear. To my mind, they openly contradict the Mishnah's teaching that one spouse may force another to move to Israel.[7] So, as emphatic as the Mishnah is about compelling *aliyah* and blocking *yeridah* for a spouse, the Babylonian Talmud commentary on the

Mishnah is more moderate in its outlook. I will return to this point later.

The Tosefta does say elsewhere that a Jew is obligated to live in Israel. Tosefta *Avodah Zarah* 4:3,4 says:

> A person should live in Israel, even in a city that is primarily non-Jewish, and not outside of Israel, even in a city that is all Jewish. This teaches that living in Israel is weighted against all other *mitzvot* of the Torah. And anyone who is buried in Israel, it is as if he is buried right under the altar. A person should not leave Israel unless wheat costs a *sela* for two *seah*....

In the broad context of discussing relationships between Jews and non-Jews in Israel, and in the more immediate context of discussing the right to hoard food and to export staples, such as wine, oil, and flour, in times of famine, the Talmud says that even if one has to live among non-Jews, it is still preferable to live in Israel.[8] This is one continuous statement, with only one verb: a person should live in Israel, even in a primarily non-Jewish environment, and not outside Israel, even in a primarily Jewish environment.

The Tosefta then says clearly and forthrightly that living in Israel is weighted against or equivalent to all the *mitzvot*. Or the Torah. That is, a Jew has an absolute obligation to live in Israel, just as he has an absolute obligation to comply with the other *mitzvot* of the Torah.[9]

It goes on to say (4:4) that the only justification for leaving is if the price of food rises very high and supplies are scarce. But R. Simon disagrees. He cites a midrash about Elimelekh, who, with Naomi and his two sons, left Israel in a time of scarcity but died of famine abroad, whereas the others who did not leave survived. The Tosefta then gives a reason why one should not move abroad—because it is inevitable that one will come to worship idols.

How was this Tosefta statement of absolute obligation to live in Israel received by the two Talmuds? Much of the material from Tosefta AZ appears not in Tractate AZ but in *Baba Batra* 90b. In the midst of a discussion of honest weights and measures, a topic raised by the Mishnah, the Gemara cites a *Baraita* about those who commit a variety of economic transgressions in a time of scarcity (such as hoarding food, lending money on interest, reducing the size of measures, and raising prices). Six other *baraitot* follow, all on this topic. Many of them are the same as those that appeared in Tosefta AZ.[10] But despite the fact that the Gemara in *Baba Batra* brings so much Tosefta material, it fails to cite the statement that living in Israel is an absolute obligation on all Jews (Tosefta AZ 4:3). That element of the Tosefta series does not appear here or anywhere else in either of the two Talmuds. Did the Babylonian Talmud deliberately leave it out? Or did it only include *baraitot* on the topic of scarcity? I cannot say.

Parts of the *Baraita* that are missing from the series in *Baba Batra* do appear elsewhere, in *Ketubot* 110b, in the course of discussing the Mishnah about forcing a spouse to move to Israel:

> Certainly a person should live in Israel, even in a city that is primarily non-Jewish. And one should not

> live outside of Israel, even in a city that is all Jewish. For anyone who lives in Israel, it is as if he has a God, and anyone who lives outside of Israel, it is as if he does not have a God, as it says.... This comes to teach you that anyone who lives outside of Israel, it is as if he worships idols.

This *Baraita,* as we saw in its Tosefta version, says that one should surely live in the land, even among idolaters, and not outside the land, even among Jews. Again, of extreme importance is the fact that the first and second lines of this *Baraita* are one continuous thought, not two separate ones, even though the verb repeats in the second part of the statement. These lines mean: Do not use living in a Gentile environment in Israel as a rationale for moving to the Diaspora. Living among non-Jews in Israel is better than choosing to live, even among Jews, outside of Israel. The second line is a restatement of the first, transposed into the negative for emphasis.[11]

Another noteworthy feature of this *Baraita* is that the second clause, as it appears in the Babylonian Talmud, is different from the second clause in the Tosefta. What has been deleted is the direct statement in the Tossefta of the obligation to live in Israel, that that obligation weighs equally with all the other *mitzvot*. Instead, the second clause of the *Baraita* gives a rationale for the first: if you live in Israel you will have a God, but if you live outside of Israel you will not.

It is hard to accept that the Babylonian Talmud was unfamiliar with the statement of absolute obligation, since virtually all the

Tosefta series of *baraitot* (Tosefta *AZ* 1–5) appears in the Babylonian Talmud, either in *Baba Batra* or in *Ketubot*,[12] except for 3b, the statement that there is an obligation to live in Israel. It therefore seems reasonable to conclude that the Babylonian Talmud intentionally deleted it.

If so, this omission suggests that the Babylonian Talmud makes a clear distinction between the obligation not to leave the land if one is already living there, even in difficult times, and the obligation to move there from abroad if that is where one was born or is living. When the Babylonian Talmud in this context says that a Jew should live in Israel, even in a Gentile environment, rather than outside Israel in a Jewish environment, it is saying that one should stay in Israel and not leave, because, even though surrounded by non-Jews, that is where God is. It does not obligate a Jew to move to Israel from the Diaspora. Were the Babylonian Talmud interested in teaching that one has to move to Israel, it would have said so explicitly. Rather, like the Mishnah, the Babylonian Talmud favors living in the land over living elsewhere but does not impose it as an absolute obligation upon someone who was born and is living elsewhere.

Immediately following this *Baraita*, the Babylonian Talmud relates that R. Zera would try to avoid meeting R. Judah, because R. Zera was planning to move to Israel and R. Judah sharply opposed *aliyah*, going so far as to say that whoever leaves Babylonia for Israel transgresses a positive *mitzvah*, for the verse says, "[T]hey will be brought to Babylonia and there they will remain until I remember them" (Jer. 27:22).[13] This extreme statement suggests that the Babylonian Jewish community was struggling with the issue of whether remaining in the *golah* transgressed a rule of the Torah and was told by its rabbinic leaders that *aliyah* was optional, at best, and possibly forbidden. Even so, R. Zera chose to leave Babylonia for Israel, as did many others.[14]

In short, if one reads the *Baraita* as I have proposed, it follows that the Babylonian Talmud does not hold that a Jew is obligated to move to Israel from the *golah*. The argument rests on the following evidence: (1) in the course of discussing a mishnah that talks about moving to Israel from the Diaspora as a favored position but does not decree an obligation to do so, the Babylonian Talmud cites Tannaitic materials that forbid leaving Israel but none that say that it is necessary to move there if living elsewhere; (2) when citing the *Baraita* about forcing one's spouse to move to or remain in Israel, it interprets it in a way that reduces the level of obligation to move to or stay in Israel; (3) and when it cites a *Baraita* about the preference for living in Israel, it omits the direct statement of obligation to live in Israel, replacing it with an argument for staying if already there. This indicates, to my mind, that the Babylonian Talmud views moving to Israel from elsewhere not as an obligation but as an option.

Nevertheless, if we now look at the rest of the Babylonian Talmud commentary on the Mishnah about moving one's spouse to Israel, we find that although not seeing *aliyah* as obligatory, it offers some rather persuasive arguments for leaving Babylonia and moving to Israel.

First, the Gemara brings a series of statements about the benefits of living in Israel: one who dwells there will be free of sin (or punishment); any one who is buried in Israel, it is as if he is buried under the altar; all those who die in Israel will come back to life in the world to come; anyone who walks four cubits in Israel is guaranteed a life in the world to come (111a).

There then follows a long series of statements about the natural abundance of the land and a glorious future in the land, and of fabulous stories from the past.

To give one example (111b): Rami B. Ezekiel once paid a visit to Bene-berak, where he saw goats grazing under fig trees. Honey flowed from the figs, milk ran from the goats, and these mingled with each other. "This is indeed," he remarked, "'[a land] flowing with milk and honey.'"

R. Jacob b. Dostai related:

> From Lod to Ono [is a distance of about] three miles. Once I rose up early in the morning and waded [all that way] up to my ankles in honey [of the figs]. Resh Lakish said: I myself saw the flow of milk and honey of Sepphoris and it extended [over an area of] sixteen by sixteen miles.

These statements may be based on some real event these rabbis experienced. But even if they are not, the underlying tone of them all is pleasure and amazement at the literal, yet fantastic fulfillment of God's promise to bring the people to a land flowing with milk and honey.

The final section of this lengthy *sugya* describes how various rabbis would act when they entered Israel from abroad (112a-b): R. Abba would kiss the stones of Akko (a city at the northern boundary); R. Hanina would repair the roads; R. Hiyya bar Gamda would roll in the dirt. These actions are all expressions of deep, abiding, and perhaps even irrational love of the land. They create a dramatic concluding flourish to the Mishnah, the chapter, and the entire tractate.

We thus see that rather than obligate a Jew to move to Israel from abroad, the Babylonian Talmud attempts to convince him to do so by providing all kinds of inducements. Giving reasons for someone to make *aliyah* functions very differently from imposing absolute obligation. In this case, a Jew is invited to think seriously about *aliyah* as an option, as a choice he or she may want to make, to review the comparative advantages and disadvantages of living in each place. As a result, anyone who decides to move will be doing so voluntarily and only after a period of profound reflection. Moreover, such a person will be able to survive periods of hardship because it was his or her own deliberate decision to go there.

When we compare the Babylonian Talmud materials on the theme of love of Israel to the Jerusalem Talmud parallels, found in *Peah* 7:3, we readily see that although the emphasis in the Babylonian Talmud is on a future of natural abundance, in real time or in the world to come, in the Jerusalem Talmud parallel a negative tone permeates the entire section: things used to be so much better than they are now; in the time of R. Yohanan, the world changed, for the worse. As for the anecdotes about kissing the land, these appear in the Jerusalem Talmud in a separate place, *Shevi'it* 4:7, in the context of a discussion of a ban on eating sabbatical produce. They seem to appear incidentally, although the sabbatical *mitzvah,* like all *mitzvot* connected to the Land, assumes the holiness of the Land.

What I am saying is that the Babylonian Talmud and the Jerusalem Talmud each contains a set of stories about the incredible abundance the Land of Israel can produce. When the Jerusalem Talmud brings these materials, it uses them as a way of saying that the present is difficult and that the past used to be much better. The *Bavli* takes the same material and puts a positive spin on it, bringing these anecdotes in conjunction with a discussion of whether to move to Israel from the *golah* and attaching to them reports about intense love of the Land. So the message to a potential *oleh* is not only can you look forward to a glorious future in terms of the Land giving forth its bounty, but you will develop a passionate love for the Land itself, as did these rabbis who felt the need to hug and kiss it each time they returned to it from abroad.

It is not surprising to me that it is only the Babylonian Talmud that developed this *sugya* on the benefits of living in the Land of Israel. The Jerusalem Talmud redactor lived in Israel in the difficult economic and political conditions of the fourth century C.E. and was unable to get beyond his own experience to read these stories for their fullest meaning. The Babylonian Talmud editor, living outside of the Land and identifying with the Jewish yearning for it as expressed daily in the liturgy, was able to read these stories of a glorious past and future in the same mode of yearning and wistfulness. It was his genius that brought together the disparate chunks of material and used them to motivate people to make *aliyah*. In short, seeing the context in which the same materials appear in each of the two Talmuds helps significantly in determining the larger message of the unit.

ALIYAH AND YERIDAH IN RABBINIC SOURCES

POST-TALMUDIC DEVELOPMENTS

Having proposed my own reading of the Tannaitic and amoraic texts on the topic of *aliyah* and *yeridah*, I will now survey just two of the post-Talmudic commentators and codists to see how they read the same texts.

1. TOSAFOT

Tosafot to *Ketubot* 110b comment, in reference to the passage "if he wants to move to Israel and she does not, he may force her to do so," that this no longer applies because the roads are dangerous. They then cite Rabbenu Hayyim who says that now we are not required to live in the Land of Israel because there are several *mitzvot* connected to the land that we will be unable to fulfill.

It is clear that the Tosafot read the Gemara as obligating a Jew to move to and live in Israel but, even so, decided that in their day moving to the land, simply from the point of view of traveling there, let alone living there, was too dangerous and therefore no longer obligatory.

2. RAMBAM

Rambam, one of the most important codifiers of Jewish law, and author of the *Mishneh Torah,* does *not* include living in Israel in the list of the 613 *mitzvot* he finds in the Torah. A close reading of his words indicates that he objects to leaving the Land but does not require one to move there: *Hilkhot Melakhim* 5:7: A person may live anywhere in the world except Egypt; 5:9: It is forbidden to leave the Land of Israel for the *golah* at any time, except temporarily for the purpose of learning Torah, finding a wife, or saving [someone] from idolaters.[15] He must then return.... But to dwell in the *golah* is forbidden unless there is a severe famine in Israel...and even in such a case it is not laudable behavior.

Rambam talks further, in 5:10, about the love various rabbis had for the Land, and then, in 5:11, lists the benefits of living in Israel. Finally, in 5:12, he says that a person should choose to live in Israel in a city that is predominantly gentile and not in the *golah* in a city that is predominantly Jewish, because for anyone who leaves Israel, it is as if he worships idols. This is all one continuous statement. He concludes the paragraph and the chapter by saying that just as it is prohibited to leave Israel for the *golah,* similarly it is forbidden to leave Babylonia for other countries.[16]

Rambam has worded his statements very carefully. His ruling is that one may not leave Israel for the *golah,* but one is not obligated, if living in the *golah,* to move to Israel. Whereas the Babylonian Talmud said that anyone who dwells in the *golah,* it is as if he worships idols, Rambam says that for anyone who *leaves* [Italics mine] Israel, it is as if he worships idols, as stated in the Tosefta 5:17. His emphasis is on not leaving Israel, not on moving to Israel from elsewhere. Since there were many verses that Rambam could have used to derive an absolute obligation to live in Israel but did not, he made the same distinction that the Gemara made: that one who is living in the land may not leave it, but one who is living elsewhere, like himself, is not under the obligation to move there.[18]

CONTEMPORARY IMPLICATIONS

Having closely analyzed these texts, one can now ask: What does all this imply about *aliyah* and *yeridah* today? One part of this question is easy to answer: *yeridah* was forbidden then, with no disputes at all, and thus remains forbidden today. What is clearly allowed is a temporary sojourn abroad for valid reasons, the most interesting one being the search for a wife (or husband).

The more challenging part of the question is whether one has to move to Israel if one was born or raised elsewhere. Although not until recently did I comb the texts for information on this matter, now, having found it, there is no simple answer.

Someone who takes Jewish history and Jewish texts seriously will conclude that moving to Israel is what a Jew is strongly encouraged to do, for a variety of reasons, some of which are the classical Zionist ones: to provide a secure homeland for Jews; promote the expression of the creative Jewish genius; live a full Jewish spiritual and cultural life; be a light unto the nations. People like me are also attracted to Israel for other reasons: the biblical view of the holiness of the Land; a desire to walk in the same places that the great and not-so-great Jews of the past walked.

Even so, many of us choose to live in the *golah*. Some try living in Israel but fail to integrate and leave. Others do not make *aliyah* because of their reluctance to accept change on matters like politics and gender issues, the lack of appropriate professional opportunities, the need to give up a shared cultural outlook, and, most poignantly, the need to leave family behind.

So, the message emerging from the rabbinic materials is: no, it is not an obligation to move to Israel, but yes, it is so highly favored that even the prevailing dominance of husbands over wives will be superseded to encourage such a move. The larger message is that moving to Israel is a decision that a person has to make for him- or herself after considering all the advantages and disadvantages. The real *mitzvah* here is to struggle and think and challenge and respond to arrive at a decision that is right for oneself. And it is precisely the notion that it must be right for the individual, that there is no simple, blanket rule, that I find so appealing. It is a brilliant tactic for the Talmud to say, on the one hand, that those who are already there are obligated to remain, and yet, on the other hand, that those who live in the *golah* are not obligated, but strongly urged, to move there. Moral persuasion is likely to be far more effective in accomplishing this goal than outright obligation.

I will end by citing the final passage of the tractate of *Ketubot* (112b): R. Hiyya bar Ashi stated in the name of Rav, an early Babylonian rabbi: In the future, even the wild trees of Israel will bear fruit. As it says, "for the tree bears its fruit, the fig tree and the vine yield their strength" (Joel 2:22). This means that a flow of blessing so powerful that it will awaken dormant talents and bring them to unanticipated and unimagined fruition is what awaits the person who moves to and lives in Israel. And this is what most of us are looking for, to live life to the fullest, to develop as many dimensions of one's intellect and psyche and spirit as one can: forging connections to God, to one's people, to the past, to the future, and to the Land. That is the promise of Israel.

ALIYAH AND *YERIDAH* IN RABBINIC SOURCES

Notes

1. The passage is found in 13:2 in the Zuckermandel version and 12:5 in the Lieberman version. The Vienna ms. reads that he may not be forced by her to move. The Erfurt ms. reads that he may. See Saul Lieberman, *Tosefta Kifshuta, Nashim* (New York: JTSA, 1967), p. 386, hereafter referred to as *TK*. Similarly, the *Bavli* version of the *Baraita* reads he *is* forced and the Yerushalmi version that he is *not* [Italics mine].

2. Lieberman, *TK* 380ff, notes that although all versions of the Tosefta read that he may be forced to move to her place of residence, this is a corruption of the text, and the Tosefta is saying that a man who marries a woman from a different part of Israel is permitted to require her to move to his part.

3. It is surprising, given the preceding clauses, that a woman, in some of the versions, may not force a man to move to Israel, since she may force him to remain if they are already there.

4. See Babylonian Talmud *Ketubot* 110b and David Halivni, *Meqorot Umesorot, Nas* (Israel: Dvir, 1968), pp. 259-260. He suggests that each of the two Talmuds had a different version of the Mishnah. The *Bavli* version implied that a wife could force a husband to move to Israel; the Yerushalmi version did not.

5. Most commentators see this *Baraita* as simply spelling out the implications of the *Baraita* in the Tosefta. Since these additions appear only here and not in the Jerusalem Talmud, I suspect that they represent a modification of the original meaning and not just an explanation. See, for example, Saul Lieberman, *TK*, p. 98. See n. 7, below.

6. See S. Y. Agnon, "Mesubin," in *Kafeh Ham Baboqer,* ed. Nurit Guvrin (Tel Aviv: Aqed, 1995).

7. Lieberman, *TK,* p. 98, comments that forcing a man to move to Israel means that if he does not want to, he may divorce her and pay the *ketubah*. I do not think it necessary to interpret the *halakhah* in the Tosefta according to the Babylonian Talmud version and in that way make all the sources agree with one another. Since the *Baraita* in the Tosefta and in the Jerusalem Talmud does not include these words, and since these words undermine the simple meaning of the passage as it appears in both the Tosefta and the Mishnah, these texts seem to disagree with each other.

8. This is reminiscent of the statement in Tosefta *Ketubot* 12:5 that a husband may force his wife to move from a city that is primarily non-Jewish to one that is primarily Jewish but not from a city that is primarily Jewish to a city that is primarily non-Jewish. That is, the statement in Tosefta *AZ* assumes the rule of the preference to live among Jews but says that living in Israel outweighs it.

9. The same statement appears in *Sifre Devarim* 80, added in from the margin, as part of two poignant anecdotes, Finkelstein edition (New York: JTSA, 1969), p. 146.

10. The second *Baraita* in *Baba Batra* is parallel to Tosefta *AZ* 4:1a, the third to 4:2, the fourth to 4:1b, and the seventh to 4:4.

11. Virtually all the codists read it as a separate, independent thought that obligates all Jews to move to and live in Israel, even those living outside the Land. I disagree with this reading, as I explain below.

12. Here the Gemara cites Tosefta *AZ* 4:3a and 5 but leaves out 3b, and in *Baba Batra* it cites Tosefta *AZ* 4:1, 2, and 4. It will also cite 3c, with the addition of a proof text, a little later in the discussion.

13. Another remarkable statement of R. Judah, cited a little later in the *sugya* is: for anyone who lives in Babylonia, it is as if he lives in the Land of Israel.

14. See Joshua Schwartz, *"Aliyah Mi-Bavel B't'Kufat Ha'Amoraim,"* Cathedra 21 (1981).

15. His Talmudic basis is: Tosefta *Moed Qatan* 1-12; Jerusalem Talmud *Berakhot* 3:1 (6a); Nazir 7:1 (56a); Babylonian Talmud *Eruvin* 47a; *AZ* 13a.

16. Rambam has reworked a Talmudic statement: the Talmud cited this verse as a proof that *aliyah* to Israel from Babylonia is forbidden. Rambam alters the derivation so that it concludes that one should not leave Babylonia for other countries, implying, of course, that in contradistinction to the view of R. Judah, one may leave Babylonia for Israel.

17. Rambam's wording is closer to the Tosefta than to the Talmud: Tosefta *AZ* 4:5 For anyone who *leaves* [italics mine] Israel at a time of peace and moves outside of the Land, it is as if he worships foreign gods.

18. It is interesting that although he states in 5:7 that one may not live in Egypt, a prohibition clearly based on verses in the Torah, he himself lived there. The Radbaz *(ad locum)* justifies Rambam's actions by saying that he was forced by the government to stay in Egypt because it needed his medical services. Alternatively, *Hagahot Maimoniyot (ad locum)* says that the only prohibition of the Torah is to move to Egypt from Israel, and Rambam did not do that.

ALIYAH: CONFLICT AND AMBIVALENCE
As Reflected in Medieval Responsa*

Moshe Zemer

liyah to the Land of Israel or emigrating from it involved innumerable difficulties with family, physical security, and *parnasah*. The decision of one member of a household to leave his or her native land and take the giant step to *Eretz Yisrael* usually had a profound effect on the rest of the family. In medieval responsa literature this decision, which often resulted in permanent separation of olim from their relatives, is usually discussed in *halakhic*, rather than emotional terms. In addition to the practical issues of an arduous journey and settling in the Land, they were confronted with a number of serious theological and *halakhic* problems.

As we shall see, this was the case of the foremost thirteenth-century *halakhic* advocate of settling in Zion. Nahmanides ruled that *aliyah*, leading to settlement in the Land, is a Torah commandment, yet he fulfilled this *mitzvah* himself only at the end of his life. Even this leading exponent of *aliyah* had to overcome a number of family obstacles and other impediments before he could practice what he exhorted.

ALIYAH OR HONORING PARENTS

Rabbi Meir ben Baruch, the Maharam of Rothenburg (1215–1293), wrote a responsum[1] about the reaction of great scholars to the mass emigration of their sons to Israel in 1211:

---
*Dedicated to the memory of Wolfram Rainer, Counsellor of the German Embassy in Tel Aviv, who died in the Land of Israel serving his government and the people of Israel.

ALIYAH: CONFLICT AND AMBIVALENCE

> You have asked if a father may prevent his son from going on *aliyah* to Israel. Since it has been established that *aliyah* to the Land of Israel is a *mitzvah*, and each such *mitzvah* is followed by "I am the Lord," which means that you should not obey your parent when he commands you to violate a *mitzvah*, because the honor due to God takes precedence.[2]

The Maharam contrasts this ruling with the behavior of great sages who opposed the *aliyah* of their children:

> You have queried if I have heard why the great sages [*gedolim*] commanded their sons to return [home to Europe]. It would appear to me that there are no merciful people there [in *Eretz Yisrael*]. The young men were unable to study Torah in the Land because they had to struggle to eke out a living. Furthermore, there was no proper guidance in Torah in the Land of Israel, nor were they proficient in the exact observance of *mitzvot*.

These sages apparently believed there was physical danger in the Land due to the cruelty of its inhabitants as well as their sons' poverty. No less threatening were the dangers of spiritual paucity in studying Torah and keeping its precepts. They were convinced that their offspring would fare much better both spiritually and physically in the Diaspora.

This conflict between parents and children about *aliyah* continued throughout the centuries. One of the great scholars who dealt with this issue was Rabbi Moses ben Joseph Trani, who was born in Saloniki, Greece, in 1490. He went on *aliyah* and became the Rabbi of Safed, where he died in 1580. He was a prolific *halakhist* who wrote innumerable responsa. The Mabit, the acronym by which he is known, received the following anonymous question:

> May our Teacher instruct us: Reuven had made a vow that, if he accumulates a certain amount, he will live in Safed, and now the condition has been fulfilled. However, his father and mother are not allowing him to go there to settle. Furthermore, his wife refuses to live there and claims that it is written in their *ketubah* that he will not take her away to live in any other place. Honoring one's father is a great *mitzvah*. Jacob our Father, of blessed memory, was punished twenty-two years [for leaving his parents]. Teach us, our Rabbi, if the vow is valid and binding or may he be released from it, and may your reward be doubled.[4]

This family dissonance results from a seemingly irreconcilable conflict between two Torah commandments: filial respect and *aliyah* to the Holy Land. If the son capitulates to his parents' demand, he will be prevented from observing the precept of dwelling in the Land.[5] If, in spite of their pleading, he does emigrate, it would appear that he was disobeying the Fifth Commandment.

Following is the Mabit's creative responsum to the inquiry:

> He neither has to fulfill his vow nor is he obligated to obey his father and mother, who told him not to go on *aliyah*, as it is taught: "If his parents told him to defile himself [where the son is a *kohen*][6] or ordered him not to return a lost animal[7] he does not obey them, for it is written: "Everyone shall fear his father and mother and

keep my Sabbaths"⁸—it is the duty of all of you to honor me, for at the end of the verse is written: 'I am the Lord.'"⁹

Using highly sophisticated Talmudic exegeses, R. Moshe Trani presents his questioner with a surprising resolution of the conflict:

> Both son and father are commanded to dwell in the Land of Israel. The son is not liable for failing to observe the *mitzvah* of honoring his parents, *because they can also go on* aliyah *with him and thereby both the commandments of dwelling in the Land and filial respect will be fulfilled.*¹⁰

We may well induce that Trani's personal life experience, no less than his knowledge of Torah, influenced this verdict. He emigrated to Safed from Turkey at the age of eighteen. From the age of twenty-one, he served on the *beit din* of R. Joseph Caro, whom he succeeded as the Rabbi of Safed. In all he lived sixty-two years in this Galilee town and served its Jewish community for more than a half century. His love of Zion was not in the abstract. It is therefore not surprising that he interpreted the *halakhah* of *aliyah* in this manner.

Halakhic decisors do not render their judgments merely from a cold analytic perspective of *halakhah,* but are influenced by their own ethical values and *weltanschauung.*¹¹

About a century before Trani, Rabbi Simeon ben Zemah Duran (1361–1444), known as the Rashbatz, approached this problem of parents, children, and *aliyah* from a different angle.¹² After hyperbolic recital of the Talmudic praises of the Holy Land, he ruled that going abroad from the Land of Israel is permitted for two purposes: (1) if a person intended to study Torah and could find no one in Palestine to teach him, or (2) to fulfill the commandment to honor one's father and mother.[13] This permission is granted only on the condition that he return to Israel, as Maimonides states: "It is forever forbidden to leave Israel for the Diaspora, except to study Torah, to marry a woman, or to effect a rescue from the Gentiles *and then he must return to the Land.*[14]

The source of this *halakhah* is apparently the Talmudic tale of Rav Assi, who left his aged mother to come to the Land of Israel. When he heard that his mother was following him, he went to R. Johanan to request permission to leave Palestine to go abroad. R. Johanan replied that it is forbidden. Assi asked, "But what if it is to meet my mother?" Johanan replied, "I don't know," but some time later said to Assi, "If you are determined to go, may God bring you back in peace." Only after Assi had left for Babylon, did he discover that his mother had died on the way to her son and that her coffin was being brought for burial in the Holy Land.[15]

Rabbi Ovadia Yosef interprets the commentary of the Maharsha (Rabbi Samuel Eliezer Edels, 1561–1631) to this passage that one is permitted to go abroad to fulfill the *mitzvah* of honoring one's father and mother only on the express condition of returning to Israel.[16]

We thus see that over the centuries the commandment of *aliyah* was considered to have precedence over filial honor. This related both to going to Israel from the Diaspora or to going on *yeridah* from the Land.

ALIYAH AND THE MARRIED COUPLE

The *halakhah* governs (or guides) a wedded pair in its decision to migrate to the Land. There is a certain symmetry in the rulings relating to man and wife as revealed in the following Tannaitic source, a *Baraita* in *B. Ketubot 110b:*

> If a man wishes to go up [to *Eretz Yisrael*] and his wife refuses, she is forced to go up. If she does not consent, she may be divorced without her *ketubah.* If the wife wishes to go on *aliyah* and he refuses, he is forced to go up; if he does not agree, he must divorce her and pay the *ketubah.*[17]

Maimonides codifies this Talmudic *halakhah* almost word for word but eliminates the use of force on the man or woman to accompany her/his spouse on *aliyah.*[18] The economic sanction against the woman involving the loss of the considerable sum in her *ketubah* or against the man who must pay this amount was apparently considered sufficient without community pressure. In any event, the Rambam rules that a woman who refuses to go up to the Land of Israel with her husband forfeits the payment of her marriage contract.

THE DECEITFUL HUSBAND

The Rambam shows how a person may misuse this *halakhic* ruling as well as his counteraction in the following responsum:

> Reuven married Leah in Alexandria and gave her a postdated bond [for her *ketubah*] in the amount of one hundred Egyptian dinars. She is a scion of an outstanding Alexandrian family. After she had borne him a son ... a quarrel broke out between the man and his wife's relatives. He swore in the presence of witnesses that she would not be his wife unless she canceled thirty dinars of his debt to her. His intention was to triumph over his in-laws. When his wife's family heard this, they were greatly incensed that he would decrease his obligation to his wife without any wrongdoing on her part. His demand was so disgraceful that they stopped her from agreeing to it. Her relatives took him to the *beit din*, where he was informed that he could not force his wife to forfeit the sum.[19]

To this point of the questioner's narrative, we are presented with a not uncommon financial controversy between members of a family. Then the husband discovers a *halakhic* artifice that will help him win the case and, suddenly, the love of Zion enters his heart. The questioner continues:

> Someone at the Rabbinical Court advised him to invite his wife to go with him to *Eretz Yisrael* and settle there. If she would not agree to leave her family and native country, she would lose the postdated bond. Therefore, she would be forced to succumb to his will. The husband threatened his spouse with this action, and made this claim in the *beit din*.

So far, the narrative of the case. Now we hear the *halakhic* verdict of the *beit din:*

> They ruled that if the way is not dangerous, and if there is no other obstacle that would prevent the journey, the woman is obligated to go to the Land of Israel and settle there. If she does not acquiesce, she will be divorced without her *ketubah*.[20]

Reuven won the court case, but the leaders of the Alexandria Jewish community were unwilling to accede to this unjust decision. They appealed to the Rambam to resolve this inequity.

The man's lawsuit was upheld. When the leaders of the community heard the verdict, however, they were extremely angry and asserted that anyone who hates his wife and wants to divorce her without the *ketubah* payment will libel her with this false charge, which would become the reason for divorcing most women from their husbands.

> May your Majestic Holiness teach us whether to acquiesce to this doubtful outcome or to return to the accepted custom of the state and what are the ramifications of this case, in accordance with his wondrous wisdom and his reward will be great.[21]

On the face of it, Maimonides might have been expected to confirm the decision of the Alexandrian judges, since it was almost identical with his own codification in the *Mishneh Torah:* "If a man wishes to go up to the Land of Israel and his wife refuses, she is to be divorced without her *ketubah*."[22]

> This is well known to us in cases adjudicated by rabbinical courts in the West,[23] which rule that any man who brings such a charge against his wife must take an oath in the Divine Name, avowing that the only reason for his action is to go on *aliyah* to find blessing in the Land of Israel, and the husband answers "Amen." Then they force the wife to go up with him or she is divorced without her *ketubah*. I have seen how these courts act.

This oath, administered by the court *(shevuat ha-dayyanim)*, has dire consequences for one who makes a false deposition. The judges warn him of immediate divine retribution for perjury under this oath in God's name.[24] Maimonides goes on to assert that these exhortations "should be taught to everyone who knows the meaning of the verses 'Justice, justice shall you pursue'[25] and 'You shall not utter a false report.'[26] The result of this is that a judge must be guided only by what his eyes see."[27] The *Dayan* must exercise his own adept judgment based on the facts of the case.

The Great Eagle (as the Rambam is often addressed)[28] presents criteria for determining a husband's creditability when he claims that he wants to go to the Land with his wife.

> A man that seeks to go on *aliyah*—who is known for his honesty and had no quarrel in any matter whatsoever with his wife—we shall require his wife to go with him to the Land of Israel. However, if one of these conditions is lacking, no verdict shall be given that she must accompany him.

ALIYAH: CONFLICT AND AMBIVALENCE

How does Maimonides apply these criteria to our case of the deceitful husband from Alexandria? We see here that he was not only an academic teacher of the Law and codifier of *halakhot*, but an administrator of justice in specific matters of case law.

> Now this "little fox,"[29] who makes this claim or another like it, is allied with criminals[30] and joins hands with wickedness. Thus it is with all those who make false charges in order to avoid an obligation that they have undertaken, like withholding the wages of an employee, which is exploitation no less than the deeds of a robber. In my mind there is no difference between one who withholds wages until the end of the day and then afterward finds some specious reason not to pay the worker and one who contrives to deprive his wife of her marriage contract.... Indeed it is easy for most men to afflict their wives to avoid paying their *ketubah*. It would be appropriate to beware of this iniquity and stop those who perpetrate it, "break the arm of the wicked and evildoer,"[31] and "rescue the oppressed from the hand of the oppressor."[32] Signed, Moshe.

The Rambam points out that most men can easily afflict their wives. They can make these poor women's lives miserable, but if the latter were to protest too much, they might be considered rebellious wives, who could be divorced without recompense. The wife is in the position of the oppressed, about whom the Torah and the Prophets were forever concerned. The Maimoni has no hesitancy in comparing this man's misdeeds with sinning against the Torah prohibition of oppressing the needy wage earner. Maimonides did not limit himself to the strict letter of the law, which he himself had codified. On the contrary, he contradicts the literal reading of his own *pesikah*.³³ Whereas code law deals with general issues for an entire population in any area, case law as revealed in the responsa literature tries to take into consideration ethical principles related to the special circumstances of a suffering individual.³⁴

THE DANGERS OF *ALIYAH*

Rabbi Samson b. Abraham of Sens, a Tosafist leader of the 300 rabbis who migrated to the Holy Land in 1211, responded to questions asked by R. Menahem, who had vowed in public that he would go up to *Eretz Yisrael*:

> The vow may be nullified, even though it was made publicly, since his wife is with child and nothing takes precedence over saving life [*pikkuah nefesh*]. It would be dangerous to make a pregnant woman travel and [take] her newborn on such a hazardous journey before the child develops and the summer arrives.... Do not rejoin that there is no danger of life here, since you could go without your wife. In no way would you be allowed to abandon her [*leag'nah*], since you are beholden to her. This is a great *mitzvah,* so therefore your vow can be nullified.³⁵

Karnafogel reasons that R. Samson's ruling would probably have been different if R. Menahem's wife had not been pregnant. The way to the Land was always very difficult, but under these circumstances mother and child were in extremely great risk. This is the narrow basis for exempting his questioner from fulfilling the *mitzvah*. He does not base his ruling on the existence of widespread danger or on the lack of a strict obligation to live in Israel, as did other medieval *poskim*. Rather, the *mitzvah merubah* of not removing his wife and son from danger or not leaving her an *agunah* was sufficient reason to nullify a publicly made vow.

The Tosafist, Rabenu Haim Cohen, completely negated the *halakhic* requirement to settle in the Land of Israel for his generation. In his commentary on the Talmudic controversy of whether couples may compel one another to go to the Holy Land,[37] R. Haim claimed that this debate was irrelevant in his day for two reasons: (1) danger and (2) the impossibility of observing *mitzvot*.

> 1. Compelling one's spouse to go to the Land may be applied only to the period when the roads are safe, but is not observed in our time because of the danger of traveling. He cannot treat her as a mere object to force her to go to a den of lions and highwaymen.[38]

> 2. In our day, one is not obligated to live in *Eretz Yisrael* because there are many commandments which must be kept in the Land and many penalties [for their neglect], of which we cannot beware or fulfill.[39]

Many pietists went on *aliyah* to observe those precepts that could be kept only in the Land. Many of these Land-bound commandments *(mitzvot ha-teluyot ba-aretz)* were related to the Temple, and others had not been kept for centuries. These laws and regulations were not fully understood. As a result, settling in the Land might result in violation rather than observance of these *mitzvot*.

Rabbi Moses B. Joseph Trani (Mabit, 1490–1580) rejected the first ruling of R. Haim for the following reasons:

At this time, one may not force a spouse or family to go on *aliyah*, because of the dangerous way for a man's wife and children. However, if the man goes alone for trade or to fulfill a *mitzvah, there is no danger even if accompanied by the family!* In our day, when the two great powers of Edom [Christian Europe] and Ishmael [Islamic Arabs] are at peace with each other, there is not very much danger. Periods of time exist during the years when you can travel to *Eretz Yisrael* from great distances. You may find people making a voyage to the Land from Italy, Germany, and France by way of the Turkish Ottoman Empire and from there to the Land of Israel. They go there even for trade, which is not obligatory, as well as for the mandatory *mitzvah* of *aliyah*. Even though bandits are occasionally on the roads, travelers, on the whole, arrive safely.[40]

Of course, Moses di Trani lived at a time removed from that of R. Haim and others who were disquieted by the dangers of traveling to and living in the Holy Land. Indeed, as we have seen,[41] his evaluation of the reality of the situation was influenced by the personal experience of having lived most of his life in Safed. He traveled abroad and received a number of visitors. Yes, there was some danger on the way, but in those days almost all travel abroad, even to a nearby destination, was hazardous. If Jews could travel to Palestine for trade and profit, how much the more could they and their families go on *aliyah*. Above and beyond all other considerations was the supreme importance of the commandment to go up and dwell in the Holy Land.

His son, R. Joseph b. Moses Trani (Maharit, 1568–1639) considered the second ruling of Rabenu Haim against *aliyah* fallacious. He contended that some agricultural *mitzvot* connected with the Land could definitely be observed in the present—that is, the Middle Ages. These included, among others, *leket* (gleanings), *shi'khehah* (the forgotten sheaf), *peah* (corner of the field left for the poor), and *ma'asarot* (tithes). Furthermore, the Maharit declared that dwelling in the Land is a positive *mitzvah* of the Torah as established by Nahmanides. He goes on to list some of the great advantages of living in *Eretz Yisrael* and concludes that the *halakhah* is well established that wherever no danger exists one is compelled to go up to the Land. In reply to a questioner, he summed up his view with the succinct determination: "Therefore, you should not heed the warnings of Rabenu Haim."[42]

The Maharit seems to have been influenced not only by his father's convictions, but by his own experiences in *Eretz Yisrael* as well. He was born in Safed and served there as a rabbi and head of a yeshivah. He had lived there for more than thirty years when, in 1639, he was sent to Constantinople on behalf of the Jewish community of Safed. He became the chief rabbi of the capital city and eventually of all Turkey. In spite of the distance, he remained in close contact with his family in the Galilee. His firsthand knowledge of the reality of the Land and its *halakhot* gave him a perspective quite different from that of his colleagues in Europe.

The Maharit ruled in a case similar to that related by R. Samson above.[43] He was consulted by a certain R. Isaac who had been vowing for two years that if his wife bore him a son he would go on *aliyah* to the Land of Israel. His wife did indeed give birth to a male child, but the next year he was unable to go. Then he left his home and family in the city of Adrianople, Turkey. He expressed himself as full of anxiety about his unfulfilled vow. He was penniless and would have become a beggar. Furthermore, he was terrified of the sea and its fearsome waves. He wished to know whether he could receive release from his vow.

R. Joseph Trani, citing R. Asher b. Yehiel as his authority,[44] states that usually one is not granted release from a holy vow to fulfill a *mitzvah*, such as going on *aliyah*. In contrast to his own exhortations just cited, he allows an exception where the route is hazardous or there is a risk that the man might leave his wife an *agunah*: in such a situation, observing the precept of *aliyah* could lead to a sin *(mitzvah goreret aveirah)*. Consequently, the man from Adrianople may be released from his vow. The Chief Rabbi of Turkey proclaimed:

> The essence of the *mitzvah* is not *aliyah*, but *dwelling* [*yeshivah*] in the Land and establishing a home there, as the late Nahmanides taught. Anyone who goes there as a tourist intending to return whence he came is not fulfilling the well-known *mitzvah*.[45]

PREACHING AND PRACTICING *ALIYAH*

Great *halakhists*, like all other human beings, were not always able to apply their *pesikah* to their own lives. Instructing their followers around the Jewish globe about the supreme value, holiness, and importance of *Eretz Yisrael* with *halakhot*, responsa, and theological tracts was one matter; drawing conclusions for themselves and putting them into action was quite another issue. A touchstone of these rabbinic judgments and teachings was whether the rabbi himself adopted them and went on *aliyah* to settle in the Land of Israel.

Maimonides (1138–1204) recorded the Talmudic statements about *Eretz Yisrael* almost literally. Did he assume these *halakhot* as a guide for his own life? He wrote in *Hilkhot Melkhim:* "One should always live in the Land of Israel, even in a city which is mostly gentile, and not outside the Land in a city that is mostly Jewish, because one who leaves for the Diaspora is like an idolater."[46] Yet, when he and his family left Spain in 1160, they migrated to Fez, Morocco. He remained there for five years until his friend and teacher, Rabbi Judah ibn Shoshan, was arrested and executed by the Moslems.

Maimonides feared that the same fate might await him, so on April 18, 1165, he fled with his family by boat for a safe haven in *Eretz Yisrael*. After a stormy voyage he arrived in Acco about a month later, on May 16, 1165.[47] He continued his work on the Mishnah commentary in Palestine and traveled to Jerusalem and other parts of the Land. At the end of 1165 or the beginning of 1166, he emigrated to Alexandria, Egypt. The entire period of his residence in the Land was slightly more than half a year.

The Rambam codified the following laws in *Hilkhot Melakhim* about leaving the Land of Israel for the Diaspora and especially for Egypt:

> It is forever prohibited to leave the Land of Israel except to study Torah or marry a woman or to save a person from the pagans or for trade, but it is forbidden to settle in the Diaspora, except if the famine there [in Palestine] is so severe that a dinar's worth of wheat is sold for two dinars. However, if the staples are inexpensive, but one has no money or possibility of earning a living and all savings have been spent, he may go to any place where he can subsist. Even

though it is permitted to leave, it would not be indicative of the quality of piety....[48]

None of these permissive circumstances seems to have applied to Maimonides' leaving the Land. There was no scholarly rabbi in Egypt who could possibly teach him Torah. Nothing is heard about any financial distress. His statement that one may leave under such circumstances but would be considered lacking *midat hasidut* (the quality of piety) was certainly not a light matter to the author of these laws.

Maimonides used this term, *midat hasidut*, to describe the conduct of one who takes it upon himself to observe beyond the letter of the law. He cites as a negative example the sons of Naomi, Mahlon and Chilion, who left the Land of Israel because of famine and died in the country of Moab (Ruth 1:1–5). Why did they die, even though it is permitted to emigrate to escape starvation?

The Rambam explains that they were the great men of their generation, and therefore they were punished by God. The source for his assertion is the Talmudic dictum in the name of Rabbi Simeon b. Yohai: "Elimelech [Naomi's husband], Mahlon, and Chilion were the great men of their generations as well as leaders of their generations *(parnasei hador)*. Why then were they punished? Because they left Palestine for a foreign country."[49]

Here is the conundrum: Maimonides is definitely considered to be among the greatest scholars and leaders of his generation. He was certainly aware when he codified these laws that they might refer to himself. He did not even have the mitigating circumstances of a famine. Furthermore, he did not merely leave the Land of Israel, but he went to settle in Egypt, which was forbidden according to his own code.[50]

It is permitted to dwell everywhere in the world except in Egypt. It is forbidden to settle anywhere in its domain, because the Torah warns us in three places not to return to Egypt:

> The Lord has said to you, "You shall never return that way again" (Deut. 17:16).
> I promised you that you shall never see (Egypt) again (Deut. 28:6).
> The Egyptians that you see today, you will never see again (Exod. 14:13).

Maimonides comments that there are certain permissible exceptions: "It is permitted to return to Egypt for trade and business or to pass through to conquer other lands. The only prohibition is to *settle* there."[51] Here lies the great difficulty. The Rambam did not go to Egypt for trade, business, or war, but to *settle* there. He does not explain this deviation from the *halakhot* that he himself codified. We may be able to find a vague hint of a futuristic *halakhic* justification for settling in the Land of the Nile, however, in his explanation in the same reference, "If a King of Israel conquered Egypt with permission of a *beit din* ... it would be permitted to settle there...." His explanation, of course, did not refer to his period of time. His style of codification is also puzzling in his comparison of leaving *Eretz Yisrael* with leaving Babylon. He concludes his laws of *aliyah* and *yeridah* with the following: "Just as it is forbidden to leave the Land of Israel, so it is forbidden to leave Babylon."[52]

All these rulings, of course, have their roots in the Talmud and related rabbinical literature, yet the juxtaposition and the emphasis are those of Maimonides. Scholars throughout the ages have tried to understand if he found any justification for violating his own *halakhic* rulings by leaving the Land of Israel and settling in Egypt.

Estori (ben Moshe) HaParhi (1280–1355), prolific chronicler and topographic researcher of the Land of Israel, characterized Maimonides' situation in Egypt in his work *Kaftor va-Ferah*.[53]

> I heard in Egypt from the late R. Samuel, a descendent of the Rambam,[54] that when Maimonides signed his name on a letter, he would add: "The writer who transgresses three negative commandments every day."

Scholars of several generations have refused to accept this evidence of the Rambam's repeated public confession. His autograph is found in original manuscripts of responsa, but never with these concluding remarks to which Estori HaParhi testifies.

Rabbi David ibn Zimri (Radbaz, 1480–1574), lived in Spain, Egypt, and the Land of Israel. In his commentary to Maimonides' prohibition to settle in Egypt, the Radbaz states: "If you should say that our Rabbi is contradicted by his own text, because he settled in Egypt, one might respond that he was compelled by the rulers, because he was physician in attendance to the Sultan and his ministers. I also lived a very long time in Egypt to study and teach Torah and even made it my domicile, which is permitted. Nonetheless, I returned to Jerusalem."[55]

The Radbaz, in his apologetic defense of the Rambam, slipped in an autobiographical note that reveals the similarity between the two scholars' establishing residency in the forbidden land. The apparent contradiction between Maimonides' ruling and his deeds is resolved by the existence of extenuating circumstances. The Rambam was forced by Egypt's rulers to remain and attend to the medical needs of its royalty. In contrast, the Radbaz remained there for the sake of Torah, which is *halakhically* permitted. But he, unlike, Maimonides, did go back to Jerusalem, where he started a second rabbinic career that lasted until the ninety-fourth year of his life.

Nahmanides (Gerona, Spain, 1195–1270) was probably the greatest and most consistent *halakhic* exponent of the Land of Israel. As we have seen, his view of the *halakhic* role of *Eretz Yisrael* had vast influence on sages in every age. This influence has continued to our day.[56] Maimonides did not establish settling the Land of Israel as a biblical precept in his *Sefer HaMitzvot*. In his gloss to Maimonides' Book of Commandments, the Ramban filled the void by claiming that settling *Eretz Yisrael* is indeed a divine commandment.

> We are commanded to take possession of the Land that God gave to our forefathers, Abraham, Isaac, and Jacob, and not to leave it to any of the Gentiles or to become desolate. God decreed: "You shall take possession of the land and settle it, for I have given the land to you to possess it" (Num. 33:53) and "you shall settle the land which I have promised to your ancestors."[57]

In his commentary to this verse, Nachmanides admits that Rashi offered a contrary interpretation, that this is merely God's *promise* to Israel and not a commandment. He contradicts his late predecessor, claiming that his, and not Rashi's, rendition is correct—"our interpretation is the essence."[58]

The Nahmani consistently interprets the Torah as commanding the People of Israel to conquer, possess, and settle the Land. The Torah chastises Israel for not fulfilling this commandment, as we see in his version of the Book of the Commandments:

> And when they did not wish to go up to the land, as it is written, "You rebelled against the word of the Lord" [Deut. 1:26]. Furthermore, you did not heed the command, which is a *mitzvah* and not merely a promise or assurance.

Further proof is given by the Bible's description of the Canaanite nations' evacuation of the Land and the chronicle of the substitute areas they received.

The Torah's narrative is supplemented by rabbinic hyperbole portraying the incomparable essence of settling in this Land.

> So the Gentiles fled before us and wandered off, as our Sages said: The Girgashites dislodged and went away, and God gave them a fair land, Africa. We, on the other hand, were commanded to enter *Eretz Yisrael* and conquer its cities and settle our people there ... as our Sages taught: "Every place that the sole of your foot will tread shall be yours...." [Deut. 11:24] [T]herefore, this conquest is obligatory in every generation. I tell you that the superlatives that our Rabbis used about settling the Land reached a peak in the declaration that "anyone who lives in the Land of Israel may be considered to have a God, but whoever lives outside the Land, may be regarded as one who has no God...."[59] These panegyric praises are derived

from the Scriptural positive precept that God commanded us to possess the Land and settle it. Therefore, this must be a Torah commandment for all generations that obligates each and every one of us, even in an age of exile, as we learn from the Talmud in many places,... "Dwelling in the Land of Israel is the equivalent of all the other *mitzvot* of the Torah."[60]

The Ramban's entire exposition is based on the premise that the Torah has divinely commanded the People of Israel to settle in the Land of Israel. Therefore, this commandment must be one of the 613 Commandments of the Torah. Maimonides left it out of his list; Nahmanides corrected his oversight.

MITZVAH VIS-A-VIS REALITY

In view of his ideological and theological stance, we might have expected that the Ramban would have shown the way to Spanish Jewry by going on *aliyah* to *Eretz Yisrael,* which he had extolled in his *halakhic* and kabbalistic writings, commentaries, and poetry.

On the contrary, we find him in his native Gerona almost all his life, first serving as its rabbi and then as the spiritual and temporal leader of the Jews of Spain, as the chief rabbi of Catalonia. Then, in his sixty-ninth year, the watershed year of 1263, King James of Aragon, at the urging of the powerful Dominicans, ordered the Ramban to engage in a disputation with the apostate Jew and now Dominican monk, Pablo Christiani. The Nahmani's conduct of the theological contest as well as his later treatise on the disputation, *Sefer HaVikuah,* aroused the wrath of the monks that initiated the debate. The Dominicans demanded that the rabbi be severely castigated. Pope Clement IV sent a bull, dated 1266 or 1267, to King James calling for

Nahmanides' punishment. Very shortly afterward, Nahmanides left Spain and went to *Eretz Yisrael*.[61]

He arrived in the port of Acco and then in Jerusalem on September 1, 1267. He was overjoyed to be in the Holy City and yet crushed by the sight of the ruins where once the Temple stood. He composed an ecstatic elegy to Jerusalem and its stones in which he expressed his joy to be in Zion and mourning for its sad state. His ambivalence reached its height with his expression of longing for his family. He celebrated his homesickness in these verses that sound as if the great champion of Zion were in exile!

> I am the man, who has seen affliction / exiled from my household / distanced from both beloved and friend / because the journey is so prolonged, / I am isolated from brothers / in a wayfarer's lodging in the desert. / I left my home / abandoned my inheritance / there I left my spirit and my soul / with sons and daughters who are as my own / are the beginning of my way / my beloved and pleasant ones / who are ceaselessly with my eye and my heart. / The honor of friends may bite like a viper, / my companions in darkness, / This appears trifling / and everything precious appears despicable.[62]

This sad longing for his family and friends in Gerona is suddenly interrupted by a love song and elegy to Jerusalem. His *halakhic* affinity to Zion found expression in love poetry to the Land. Perhaps he was bolstering himself in his loneliness by recalling the realization of his great dream of witnessing the sites of the Holy City, about which he had written most of his life. So he sings to the rubble of Jerusalem:

ALIYAH: CONFLICT AND AMBIVALENCE

> How good it is for me to be one day in your courtyard / to visit your ruined, desolate Sanctuary / to see, to cherish your stones and to pity your dust/ to lament over your ruins, / for your dust in my mouth is as honey and sweets / and I shall weep over you in the bitterness of my soul and delight in lamentation.[63]

This conflict between love of family and love of the Holy Land was not resolved. The last three years of his life, Nahmanides lived without his wife and children, dying in 1270. His poetry as well as his letters to his two sons, Nahman and Shlomo, give evidence of the ambivalence between his love for the members of his family and for the land of his ancestors, which could not be reconciled.[64]

No evidence seems to have been found of why the Ramban's family did not voyage with him to the Land. We do not know if he had enough time to prepare for their departure. He had long known the Dominicans' enmity. Did he have a contingency plan to escape, as did many of his countrymen? Could the family have joined him in *Eretz Yisrael* at a later date? Were his wife or any of his children willing to risk the voyage or life in the desolate Land to be with their beloved husband and father? Did he ask them to come, or perhaps did he insist that they remain in Spain? The sources are silent and so must we be.

We have seen in our exploration of the responsa and other literature the not infrequent conflict between *aliyah* and family. At times the conflict was resolved by the family going together to the Holy Land or remaining in the Diaspora. In some cases the families separated, with one or more going on *aliyah* or *yeridah* and the rest remaining where they were. When only a small minority immigrated to the Holy Land, they were apparently either pietists or those searching for a refuge, which Palestine could not always offer.

Why was it that, in spite of the love for Zion, when the opportunity arose to settle in the Land, the vast majority, including those that preached and taught and composed poetry to express this love, remained in the land of their birth?

Yehudah Halevi (Rihal, 1075–1141), was probably the most celebrated philosopher and poet of Zion in medieval times. Yet, in his Book of the Kuzars, he gives voice to this eternal ambivalence between love for the Holy Land and the inability or unwillingness to requite this love.

In the dialogue between the King of the Kuzars and the rabbi *(Haver)*, the latter describes in detail the many verses of the Bible and the rulings of the rabbis regarding the supreme importance of the Holy Land.

The Kuzari replies: "If this be so, you fall short of the duty laid down in your own Torah, by not endeavoring to reach that place to make it your abode in life and death. Although you pray daily, 'Have mercy on Zion for it is the house of our life,' and believe that the *Shekhinah* [God's presence on earth] will return there,.. is it not 'the gate of heaven'? All nations agree on this point. Christians believe that the souls are gathered there and then lifted to heaven. Islam teaches that it is the place of ascent of the prophets.... Your fathers had no other desire than to settle in the Holy Land. They did not leave it in times of dearth and famine except by God's permission."

What could the rabbi respond to this castigation of the Gentile ruler, who clearly saw the contradiction between what was taught and what was accomplished? Were there any excuses he could offer? Was there a justification for not fulfilling the biblical precepts and rabbinic injunctions. Yehudah Halevi makes no attempt to excuse of justify this sin of omission. Rather, his rabbi candidly retorts:

> You have uncovered the Achilles' tendon of my disgrace, O King of the Kuzars![65]

After years of planning and vacillation, in 1140 Yehudah finally left for the Holy Land. The famous legend relates that the Rihal arrived in *Eretz Yisrael* and Jerusalem, where he kissed its ruins and recited his famous elegy, "Zion, will you not ask about the welfare of your prisoners?" While in this act, a Moslem horseman trampled him to death.[66] In reality, Jerusalem was under Crusader rule at this time, so this story can be only legendary.

Reality in contrast to myth was not so romantic. Yehudah Halevi arrived in Alexandria on September 8, 1140, and was received by a crowd of admirers. He sojourned for quite a while in the port city and then in Cairo. His close friends and disciples tried to influence him to remain longer in Egypt. At one point he went to the port of Alexandria to take a boat to the Holy Land, but a storm prevented its sailing. *Genizah* letters and eulogies indicate that about six months after his arrival he died and was buried in Egypt.[67]

This tragic, ironic finale to the life of this great savant of Zion indicates that even on the verge of realizing his ultimate desire, he failed to take the ultimate step and ended his life in exile.

AFTERWORD

What do we learn from these successful and failed attempts to go on *aliyah* and settle the Holy Land? We find that they involved not only *halakhic* and theological polemics, but very pragmatic issues as well.

1. PARENTS AND CHILDREN—On the *halakhic* level, was *aliyah* a commandment that was incumbent on Jews in the Middle Ages? Most *halakhists* ruled that this *mitzvah* overruled even the Fifth Commandment of honoring one's parents. Among those who so determined the *halakhah* were the Maharam of Rothenberg, of the thirteenth century, and Moses Trani, of the sixteenth century. The former made his ruling against that of the great sages who settled in the Land a generation before. Later on they sent their sons back home to Europe, because of the difficult conditions in the Holy Land relating to cruel inhabitants, unemployment, and lack of Torah guidance. The Rashbatz (1361–1444) took a middle position, allowing a resident of Palestine to go abroad to study Torah or to honor his parents, on the proviso that he return to the Land.

This conflict between the generations is not asserted in terms of loving versus leaving parents. There is no expression of painful separation vis-à-vis independence, though these were undoubtedly very much present. On the verbal and written level we find this to be a conflict of *mitzvot: aliyah* or honoring parents. The Mabit had the perfect solution to the conflict—the young man should take his parents with him on *aliyah*.

2. MAN AND WIFE—Even though Talmudic law determined that a man could force his wife to go with him to the Holy Land, he was not permitted to use this ruling to swindle his wife. Neither could he force his wife and children to come with him to Palestine if the journey was hazardous. R. Haim said there was no longer any such *mitzvah*,

because of the dangerous trip and the impossibility of observing the agricultural commandments in the Land. Against him were aligned the Mabit and his son, who claimed that in their time, three hundred years later, the superpowers were at peace and one could join convoys from any number of European countries to the Land of Israel. This is a continuation of the debate whether one could study Torah and observe *mitzvot* better in the Holy Land or in the Diaspora. Throughout this essay, we have witnessed the pluralistic views of medieval times.

3. RABBINIC TEACHING AND APPLICATION—Three great rabbinic leaders of the twelfth and thirteenth centuries taught about the importance of *aliyah*. Maimonides codified Talmudic *halakhot* that instructed his readers to go up to the Land and to avoid returning to Egypt. Maimonides did not treat this as a biblical commandment, but rather as a rabbinic precept. He found a way of explaining away the Talmudic dictate in his responsa, as he has done in a number of instances.[68] He codified according to *halakhic* standards with which he may or may not have agreed. When he dealt with case law of individuals, the acute situation at times called for a radical departure from these standards.

So it appears to have been the situation in his own life. He went to the Land of Israel only as a sanctuary from persecution and possibly execution in Morocco. He spent six months or so touring the Land and then descended to Egypt. Nowhere does he try to justify this action, except for possible veiled hints.

Nahmanides wrote everything about Zion and the commandment to settle there that Maimonides had left unwritten. He wrote and he preached, but he remained in Spain. Only when his life was in danger, in the aftermath of the disputation, did he leave alone for his spiritual homeland. Here, at the age of sixty-nine, he was in exile from his beloved household, writing lamentations to the ruins of Jerusalem and to the distant family he was never to see again.

Were his ardent compositions about *aliyah* merely academic, meant to influence others, but not for him or his family to take seriously? Was this a matter of teaching *lehalakhah ve-lo lema'aseh* (in theory but not in practice)? Was he, like many others, so involved in his creative life in the Diaspora that he didn't make any serious plans for settling the Land with his family? The last three years of his life were fulfilling, but empty. He was in Zion, but alone.

Perhaps, the Rihal was the most sorrowful. After a lifetime of singing to Zion, he finally made the decision and began his pilgrimage. He was a tragic figure, like the biblical Moses who was commanded by God to view the Promised Land from Pisgah but not to cross over. So Yehudah Halevi stopped just short of realizing his lifelong dream. His Pisgah was Alexandria, but it was not God who commanded him to remain there. For about half a year he remained in Egypt, just a short journey from Palestine. Something in his own psyche prevented him from consummating his coveted aspiration.

The cases presented in this essay show the inner conflict of those who wish to go settle in the Holy Land. It is not surprising that the would-be *olim* might be ambivalent about leaving their family and familiar surroundings, abandoning the comforts of their native environs, to undertake an arduous and often dangerous journey to a land known to them only in holy books. How could they make a livelihood for their family, study Torah, and observe the obscure commandments connected only with the Land? Would they find a Jewish community like the one they left back home?

ALIYAH: CONFLICT AND AMBIVALENCE

It is therefore not surprising that the vast majority of those who considered *aliyah*, from the immortal medieval rabbis to famous Zionists of our own day, remained in the Diaspora. It is remarkable, however, that a number of Jews in almost every era surmounted these obstacles, left the country of their birth, and went up to the unknown Land, like Abraham, their father, and Sarah, their mother, before them.

Notes

1. Responsa *Maharam ben Barukh* (Berlin: 1891), no. 79. See also E. Karnafogel, "The *Aliyah* of 300 Rabbis," *Jewish Quarterly Review* 86 (3): 191–215.

2. This is based on *Baba Metziah* 32a, which states that one may not obey a parent's command to commit a transgression.

3. *Responsa Maharam*, ad loc. See Israel Schepansky, *Eretz Yisrael in the Responsa Literature* (Hebrew) (Jerusalem: 1966), p. 120, who states that the Maharam may have been asked about the sons of those *gedolim* that lived in the generation before him who themselves went on *aliyah* to the Land. They either permitted or commanded their sons to return home.

4. *Responsa Mabit* (Lemberg: 1861), (1) 139. Mabit was one of the four Safed rabbis who received the controversial *semhah* from Jacob Berab in 1538. The others were Joseph Caro, Moses Cordovero, and Joseph Sagiz.

5. There is a difference of opinion among sages whether *aliyah* and *yeshiva ha-aretz* are Torah *mitzvot*, that must be observed "in our time," i.e., the Middle Ages. Among these who considered them obligatory under Scriptural Law was Nahmanides (see infra note and the chapters in this volume by John Rayner, notes 18–19; Leonard Kravitz, notes 33–34; and Aviezer Ravitzky, notes 30–33.

6. Leviticus 21: 1ff.

7. Deuteronomy 22:1.

8. Leviticus 19:3.

9. B. *Yevamot* 6a. See also supra, note 2.

10. *Responsa Mabit*, ad loc. (supra, note 4; emphasis mine).

11. See Moshe Zemer, *Halakhah Shefuyah* (Tel Aviv: Dvir, 1993), on Maimonides, pp. 26–28; on the Rama, pp. 29–32; on R. Yehudah Leib Zirelsohn, pp. 79–81; and many other respondents

who rendered their decisions in this way. Also, note idem., "Purifying Mamzerim," *Jewish Law Annual* 10 (1992): 99-114, for the influence of individual value systems on rabbinic decisions.

12. The Rashbatz was born in Majorca in 1361 and died in Algiers in 1444. He served as chief rabbi and head of the rabbinic court in Algiers.

13. *Responsa Tashbetz* (Lemberg: 1891), (3) 288. See also the responsum of R. Samson b. Zadok to the question: "Why didn't all the Amoraim go up to the Land?" To this he responded: "They had no financial support, so they were forced to relinquish their Torah studies to pursue a livelihood. If it is permitted to leave the Land to study Torah, how much more should one not leave his Rabbi in the Diaspora to go to *Eretz Yisrael* and neglect his studies in order to search for a way to make a living." *Responsa Tashbetz (Katan)* (Lemberg: 1858), No. 561.

14. *Hilkhot Melakhim* 5:3 (emphasis added).

15. B. *Kiddushin* 31a-b.

16. *Responsa Yehaveh Da'at* (Jerusalem: 1978-84), (4):49.

17. See the other sources in M. *Ketubot* 13:11 and *Tosefta Ketubot* 13:2. See the chapter in this volume by Judith Hauptman on "*Aliyah* and *Yeridah* in Rabbinic Sources" and the chapter by Leonard Kravitz, "Israel and the Diaspora—Sacred and Profane," which analyze these and other sources on these problems.

18. *Hilkot Ishut* 13:19.

19. *Teshuvot Ha-Rambam* (Blau edition) (2), No. 365.

20. The court relied on the Mishnah and the Gemara in B *Ketubot* 110b and *Tosefta Ketubot* 12:5.

21. Ibid. (supra no. 19); [italics].

22. Supra no. 18 [italics].

23. The lands of North Africa that are west of Egypt. See Blau (supra note 19) (2): 162, p. 310, note 3. Other references are found in idem., responsa 70, 113, 143, et al.

24. *Hilkhot Shavuot* 16:11.

25. Deuteronomy 16:20.

26. Exodus 23:1.

27. B. *Baba Batra* (1) 10a. See Rashi ad loc. The Rambam in his *Hilkhot Sanhedrin* 24:3 explains how the *Dayyan* can distinguish between truthful and deceitful litigants and witnesses.

28. See *Teshuvot Ha-Rambam* (supra 19) no. 311 et al.

ALIYAH: CONFLICT AND AMBIVALENCE

29. Song of Songs 2:15—"The little foxes that spoil the vineyards."

30. *B. Gittin* 61a.

31. Psalms 10:15.

32. Based on Jeremiah 21:12.

33. Supra no. 22.

34. My monograph, *The Lesser Evil, A Maimonidian Halakhic Technique*, which is due for publication in 1997, deals in length with this issue.

35. R. Samson's responsum is found in *Responsa Maharam* (4) 202; see supra note 1.

36. Karnafogel (supra note 1), pp. 198-200.

37. See supra note 17.

38. *Hagahot Mordecai* 312 to *Ketubot;* cf. *Tosfot Ketubot* 110b, s.v. *hu omer*, where this view is anonymous.

39. Ibid. *Tosfot Ketubot* 110b.

40. *Responsa Mabit* (supra note 4) (3), 131. [Italics].

41. Supra notes 10-11.

42. *Responsa Maharit* (Lemberg: 1861) (1), 131. See the ruling of his father, the Mabit, R. Moses b. Joseph Trani (supra notes 4-11).

43. Supra note 35.

44. *Responsa HaRosh* 12:7.

45. *Responsa Maharit* (supra note 40) (2), 28.

46. *Hilkhot Melakhim* 5:12, based on *b. Ketubot* 110b. The author does not mention the Talmudic statement that immediately precedes this: "For anyone who lives in the Land of Israel, it is as if he has a God; and anyone who lives outside the Land, it is as if he had no God...." See, in contrast, Nahmanides, infra, note 53.

47. See Solomon Zeitlin, *Maimonides* (New York: 1955), pp. 5-15; David Yellin and Israel Abrahams, *Maimonides, His Life and Works*, 3rd ed. (New York: 1972), pp. 24-38.

48. *Hilkhot Melakhim* 5:9.

49. *B. Baba Batra* 91a.

50. *Hilkhot Melakhim* 5:7.

51. Ibid. 5:8 (emphasis added). As we have seen (supra 48), the Rambam permitted one to leave the Land of Israel to study Torah abroad, which was considered a temporary matter. It is unlikely that Maimonides could have found anyone in Israel who could have served as his mentor.

52. Ibid. 5:12.

53. *Kaftor va-Ferah* (Jerusalem: 1994), Chap. 5, pp. 81-83.

54. Ibid., p. 81, conjectures that this might have been R. Samuel ben R. Solomon ben R. David HaNagid, but gives no evidence for this identification.

55. Radbaz, Commentary to *Mishneh Torah, Hil. Melakhim* 5:7.

56. See *Responsa Maharit* (supra note 44). For an example of his continuing influence, see Rabbi Nahum Rabinowitz, "The *Mitzvah* of Settling the Land," *Gilyon Rabanei Yesha* 28, Samaria, October 1995.

57. Nahmanides' gloss to *Sefer HaMitzvot* (Jerusalem:1957), positive precept 4, p.42.

58. Nahman ben Moshe, *Commentary to the Torah*, ed. by H.D. Chavel, Vol. 2 (Jerusalem:1960), p. 355.

59. *B. Ketubot* 110b. See supra, note 45.

60. *Tosefta Avodah Zarah*, ed. by M.S. Zuckermandel (Jerusalem: 1963); *Sifrei*, ed. by L. Finkelstein (New York:1969), 80:29. This is the conclusion of the Ramban's gloss to *Sefer HaMitzvot*. See supra, no. 57.

61. Israel Ta-Shema, "Moses ben Nahman," *Encyclopedia Hebraica* (Jerusalem-Tel Aviv: 1972), Cols. 565-66; see Martin A. Cohen, "Reflections of the Text and Context of the Disputations of Barcelona, *HUCA* 35 (1964), 157-92, which shows that both sides claimed victory.

62. Abraham Ya'ari, *Journeys of Jews to the Land of Israel* (Hebrew) (Ramat Gan: 1977), p. 77 (my translation).

63. Ibid. Nahmanides' verses have many allusions to biblical and rabbinic literature, with which his reader must be acquainted to fully understand his poetry.

64. H.D. Chavel, *The Writings of the Ramban* (Jerusalem: 1963), Letters 7 to Nahman and 8 to Sholomo, pp. 367-71.

65. Yehudah Halevi, *The Kuzari*, ed. by Yehudah Even Shmuel (Jerusalem: 1973), Vol. 2, 22, pp. 61-63.

66. This legend is first mentioned in Gedalya iben Yihya's *Shalshelet Hakabbalah* in the sixteenth century. See Israel Levine, "R. Yehudah Halevi," *Encyclopedia Hebraica* 19:187-88.

67. Ibid.

68. See supra no. 19; responsum 311; and my treatment of this subject, supra no. 34.

THE PRIMACY OF THE DIASPORA

Walter Jacob

Judaism contains many contradictions, but none has been as glaring as the status of Israel through the ages. The entire Jewish world celebrates a cycle of holidays agriculturally and historically connected with the Land of Israel. We orient our synagogues toward Jerusalem. We read the Torah, which moves the people of Israel gradually to the "Promised Land." We pray for the restoration of Israel and the Temple in our synagogue and home liturgies. We have supported Jews who have chosen to live in Israel through the millennia, yet most Jews for the last twenty-five hundred years have lived and continue to live in the Diaspora. This generally was by choice and design, as it is now. What role does Israel play in our Jewish existence? What is the basis for Jewish life outside the Land of Israel? Does the tradition demand *aliyah* and settlement in Israel or is this a matter of indifference? The issue may be viewed from many perspectives, but this essay will limit itself to *halakhah,* that reflects a reality of Jewish life. We shall begin with a brief summary of our biblical past.

The gift of the Land of Israel was a promise God made to the patriarchs (Gen. 12:7; 15:7, 18; 26:3; 28.4, 13; 35:12), and it remained a goal during the long period of wandering in the desert. Through the Exodus from Egypt, this was expressed as movement toward the "Land of milk and honey," a land in which God would be served at appropriate religious centers (Exod. 3:8, 6:8, 20:12; Deut. 7:1-2, 9:1-5, 25:15, 30:20, etc). The Torah clearly outlined the nature of the Land and the life to be established there, along with a centralized priestly ritual. The Land itself would be subject to the Sabbatical and the Jubilee Years. The goal of that good land was mentioned constantly and held before the people so that they would be able to endure the difficult forty-year sojourn in the desert.

We must note, however, that whereas the Exodus from Egypt continued to be celebrated through the festival of Pesah and became a focus of Jewish thought, nothing akin to that occurred with the entry into the Promised Land (Josh. 1:2-3, 24:13). Joshua simply entered and conquered, but this was never noted on our religious calendar. Furthermore, the book of conquest and settlement, the Book of Joshua, remains among the most neglected books of the Bible. Except for a single *Haftorah* reading, it has never been brought to the attention of the average Jew; it has remained a historical record.

The Land was the center of life in 1, 2 Samuel and in 1, 2 Kings; the prophets saw it as part of the divine covenant. Israel had often failed to keep its portion of the agreement. The historical and prophetic writing emphasized the need for religious conduct for Israel's leaders whether judges or kings. Rulers would be removed from power for social injustices and idolatry. Their subjects would suffer similar punishment (1, 2 Sam.; 1 Kings). The people would be exiled if they did not worship God or carry out the ethical and moral ideals the prophets expressed. Exile from the Land of Israel was seen as a divine punishment for disobedience (Elijah, Elisha, Amos, Hosea, Isaiah, Jeremiah, Ezekiel, etc).

The prophetic books also took us on the road to an idealized state in which the normal problems of statecraft were shunted aside. The later chapters of Isaiah carried this to its natural conclusion with an idealized future life without the compromises of daily life (Isa. 40:1ff).

As the people went into exile, the prophets spoke of a restoration of the kingdom and a return from foreign lands. The beautiful vision was presented in idyllic form, as the Messianic dream. A perfect descendent of David would eventually rule over a peaceful land in which everyone lived in harmony, in security, and with plenty. This kingdom would be established not by human beings, but by God (Joel 3, 4; Mic. 4; Zech. 14; Mal 3; Isa. 40:1; Jer. 3:14-18; Ezek. 37).

THE GROWTH OF THE DIASPORA

This dream continues to inspire us; in our *Haftorah* readings we have always balanced it with prophetic denunciations that dealt with the real land and its social problems. By the end of the biblical period, the people of Israel had begun to differentiate between the idealized state and their own day-to-day existence. The ideal state was left to the Messianic Age, and the vast majority of Jews decided to continue their life in Babylonia (Ezek.; Ezra 2:64) or in Egypt[1] rather than return to rebuild Israel.

We do not know how quickly the Diaspora expanded around the eastern Mediterranean, but by the time of the Maccabees,[2] there were a considerable number of communities, and that number increased significantly by the first century of our era.[3] The destruction of Judea during the various wars with Rome led to a vast expansion of the Diaspora throughout the Roman Empire.[4] The Babylonian community that soon emerged on the scene full grown and able to assume leadership must have been substantial. Within a few generations it assumed intellectual leadership along with what remained in northern Israel. Although scholars and others moved easily back and forth between Babylonia and Israel while compiling

THE STATUS OF THE LAND OF ISRAEL

the Talmud, there was no pressure to resettle Israel, even when this might have been possible. The intellectual dominance of the great academies of Babylonia and, eventually, of their Talmud spoke to the dominance of the Diaspora community over Israel.

THE STATUS OF THE LAND OF ISRAEL

Many statements in the Mishnah and the Tosefta make clear the sacredness of the Land of Israel. A series of verses in *Mishnah Kelim* indicated that "[t]here are ten degrees of sacredness. The Land of Israel is holier than any other land" and then moved upward to the "Holy of Holies" in the Temple (1.6ff). *Avodah Zarah* in the Tosefta accompanied such thoughts with a demand for settlement in Israel: "One should preferably live in the Land of Israel, even in a town with a majority of Gentile inhabitants, rather than outside the Land, even in a town in which most inhabitants are Jews...." (4.3ff; *Ket.* 10b). The Talmud rarely discussed this matter.[5] The teachers of the Mishnah, who themselves lived in Israel, encouraged settlement, but only mildly. When faced with the economic problems of farmers, they decided that the various impositions such as tithes, first fruit, and the Sabbatical and the Jubilee Years were obligatory only in the Land of Israel.[6] Furthermore, they narrowed the boundaries of Israel to a minimum to avoid hardships, discussing the various border lands and declaring most areas exempt.[7] The Talmud continued these discussions.[8] Later, more abstract discussions would dwell on whether the holiness of the Land stemmed from the patriarchs, Joshua's conquest, or Ezra's later resettlement.[9] Only a single reference elevated "dwelling in the Land of Israel above all other *mitzvot*" (*Sifrei R'eh,* Deut. 12:29). Otherwise, living in Israel was considered blessed, as was burial there (*Ket.* 111a).

Medieval philosophers and mystics continued the discussion of the special status of the Land and its intrinsic holiness; some saw it as the center of the earth.[10] A Talmudic statement considered prophecy to be limited to the Land (*M.K.* 25a), as did Yehudah Halevi (*Kuzari* 1.12).

The Talmud had already questioned whether the Land of Israel retained its sanctity after the destruction of the Temple; for the Babylonian Talmud, Babylonia was a legitimate center for Jewish life. The *Shekhinah* was seen as moving with the people of Israel wherever they went (*Sifrei B'haalotkha* 84; *Meg* 29a). Whether the *Shekhinah* favored one center of learning over another was discussed; there was general agreement that It was present in the synagogue. Some moved the entire question to the distant future, so Eleazar Hakaffar stated that "*in time* [Italics mine] the schools and synagogues of Babylonia would be planted in Israel" (*Meg* 29a). Other Talmudic statements insisted on the centrality of Israel by claiming that those who lived outside Israel had no God (*Ket.* 110b). The discussion continues through the centuries, often modified to refer only to the period of the Temple but not to the present (as Rashi [Gen. 17:8]) or to refer only to those who left Israel (as Maimonides [*Yad Hil. Melakhim* 5.12]).

The theological position already taken by the prophetic literature of the Bible was echoed in the rabbinic writings. Some scholars saw exile from the Land of Israel as divine punishment for Israel's sins. God would decide when redemption became possible, and God would bring us back; action on the part of the community was unnecessary and not to be encouraged. In other words, the condition of Diaspora was considered normal until the "end of days."

THE PRIMACY OF THE DIASPORA

A variety of Talmudic and Midrashic sources commented in this direction.[11]

MEDIEVAL REALITY AND THE LAND OF ISRAEL

Let us now see how the various attitudes toward the Land of Israel affected the Jewish relationship with that land. To what degree was resettlement practiced? What were the efforts over the centuries to make the "holiness" of the Land once more part of Jewish life and to give reality once more to the *mitzvot* that depended on the Land.

Until the days of Islamic domination of the Near East, settlement in Israel was dangerous and so could be discounted. The Byzantine rulers from the time of Helena, the mother of Constantine (ca. 324–337 C.E.), had turned the mountain on which the Temple stood into a refuse dump.[12] The prohibition against Jewish pilgrimages to Jerusalem and, of course, settlement there had been enforced from 135 C.E.) to the Arab Conquest in 638 C.E. During this long period, however, Jews had settled in small numbers in Gaza, Tiberius, and elsewhere in the Land of Israel.[13] Islamic control meant that all these areas were once more open to pilgrimages and settlement. The Omayyad (661–750) and Abbasid (750–1100) rule established an economic zone stretching thousands of miles, which provided stability for trade, travel, and population movement. Even after the fall of the Abbasids, for many centuries it was still relatively easy to travel between Islamic lands. This meant that the Land of Israel was accessible to Jews. Pilgrimages to the Land from the great Islamic Jewish centers and from the smaller

European centers were frequent.[14] Jews were also buried there from time to time, especially in Hebron, the burial site of the patriarchs.[15] *Aliyah* remained infrequent, however, except among Karaites, who propagandized for it and were motivated by Messianism, and for small waves of immigration from Islamic lands. Rabbinic Jews came only in small numbers.[16] In the Gaonic responsa, and those slightly later, were some questions about the *mitzvah* of *aliyah* and the right of a husband to force an unwilling wife to settle in the Land of Israel or to remain there, but the number of such questions is small.[17] This was not a matter of major concern, nor were other questions raised about the Land of Israel except as isolated incidents. The Talmudic statement was misused by husbands who sought to avoid *ketubah* payments by threatening to force their wives to move to Jerusalem; Maimonides therefore tested such husbands through a ban of excommunication and the need for a general reputation of honesty before he permitted it. He thus repudiated the Talmudic law.[18]

The conquest by the Crusaders destroyed all Jewish settlement, but their rule did not last long; then Muslims were in control once more. Some Jews, like Yehudah Halevi, felt a longing for the Land, but few settled there even when harsher conditions elsewhere led to some emigration. The Jews of neighboring countries like Egypt visited as pilgrims or for commerce but did not settle, although a major community there followed the guidance of the Yeshiva of Jerusalem.[19] Trade, with constant visits of merchants, continued throughout the centuries, but settlement in the Land of Israel remained rare.

The first larger group of which we hear in the Middle Ages comprised three hundred rabbis from medieval France who moved to the Land of Israel. The numbers mentioned were probably vastly exaggerated, but a significant number of scholars did settle there.[20] Their motivation may have been a desire to fulfill the commandments dependent on the Land or the Messianic prophecy. Yet the same Tosafists who had moved later commanded their sons to leave Israel and return to France, where they could study Torah more readily.[21] In any case, there was nothing like it earlier or later. Interestingly enough, a Tosafist, R. Haim Cohen, provided a rationale for the Diaspora by stating that the dangers of the journey relieved all Jews from the *mitzvah* of *aliyah*. Furthermore, Jews did not need to go to the Land of Israel because of the present dangers and because we could not execute those *mitzvot* dependent upon the Land that could not be fulfilled until the Temple was restored *(Tosfot* to *Ket* 110b). This statement commented on a Talmudic section that dealt with the right of a husband to force all the members of his household to settle in Jerusalem. Later, R. Shelomoh b. Aderet, while acknowledging the importance of *aliyah,* listed all the reasons for not following this *mitzvah,* as other factors were more important. He listed Torah study, various family reasons, and other serious problems for not making *aliyah.*[22] Other tenth-century Tosafists agreed with R. Cohen.[23]

The first medieval scholar to make resettlement in the Land of Israel primary among all *mitzvot* was Nahmanides (1194–1270). He vigorously denounced Maimonides' failure to include this *mitzvah* among the 613; for him it was more important than all the rest.[24] He stressed this *mitzvah* as well in other writings, most forcefully in a lengthy lecture for Rosh Hashanah. Despite these feelings, Nahmanides himself settled in the Land of Israel only at the end of his life, living his last three years there. A major controversy followed, partially about this issue but more about

Nahmanides' general critique of Maimonides. Nothing practical came from Nahmanides' statement. No rabbinic scholar in the *Ashkenazic* or *Sephardic* world propagandized for settlement in Israel. The statement undoubtedly encouraged those who lived there, but it had no other effect.

When Alfas (1013-1103) created his major *halakhic* code, he omitted legal material connected with the Temple and the Land of Israel. This was the first successful and influential effort at codification. Moses Maimonides (1135-1204), on the other hand, followed a different path and included all those laws, either because he wished to present a complete code or because he sought to express his Messianic longings in this fashion. Scholars continue to debate the reason. Although he spent most of his life in Egypt, Maimonides made no attempt to visit the Land of Israel; after his death he was buried in Tiberias. We should also note that Maimonides warned the Jews of Yemen against following a false Messianic leader who sought to resettle them in the Land of Israel *(Iggeret Yemen)*.

In this matter most codes followed the pattern Alfasi set, as they, too, omitted the priestly material and the laws connected with the Land of Israel.[25] Each of them sought to simplify access to Jewish learning and the religious life, as the Talmud proved to be too difficult for the average Jew. The codes provided the means by which every Jew could create a Jewish life. Along with erudite discussions, they omitted the vast aggadic material of the Talmud and laws connected with the Land of Israel of only Messianic interest and of no practical concern to the average Jew. The same pattern was followed by the summary of medieval piety expressed by the *Sefer Hasidim,* contemporary with the Crusades; it did not deal with

THE PRIMACY OF THE DIASPORA

the *mitzvah* of resettling in the Land of Israel and only once mentioned the "land" in connection with *tzedakah* (No. 1041).

The most popular major code, which continues to play a role in contemporary Jewish life, Joseph Caro's *Shulhan Arukh,* with Moses Isserles' *Mapah,* did not deal with the Temple or the Land of Israel. Caro and Isserles sought to create a practical work for the daily life of contemporary Jews.

The *Sephardic* community of the Mediterranean basin as well as the *Ashkenazic* community of Central and Eastern Europe followed this pattern illustrated by the responsa literature as well as by biblical and Talmudic commentaries of the late Middle Ages. The responsa of this period occasionally dealt with an individual who is resettled in Israel or with the *minhagim* of the Land of Israel, but the orientation was essentially toward the Diaspora.[26] This three-volume work contains all the relevant material; as one-third of it is from the last two centuries, we can see the limited inquiries made in the preceding thousand years.

We should also remember that when the Jewish community of Spain was forced into exile in 1492, although many settled in Turkey, Italy, and other parts of the Mediterranean, very few returned to the Land of Israel. The economic conditions there were not appealing; religious fervor, however, could have overcome that objection.

Jewish mysticism often stressed Messianism and therefore the Land of Israel. The mystics who settled in Safed attracted followers and brought about a small immigration to Israel; some mystics considered living in the Land the only way to attain a perfect Jewish life. This concept played a major role in the thought systems of R. Ezra ben Solomon (thirteenth century) and Abraham Abulafia (1240-1291), but not of all mystics. Individuals did not hesitate to move back to the Diaspora for various reasons, and *aliyah* was not part of all systems.[27]

The *halakhists* of Safed made an effort in the sixteenth century to reconstitute the Sanhedrin and to reestablish rabbinic ordination. This was intended to help solve a variety of *halakhic* problems that needed legislation rather than interpretation. It may also have represented an effort to affirm the primacy of the Land of Israel. In any case it aroused much objection, and the effort was speedily abandoned.

THE REFORM MOVEMENT

The nineteenth century brought dreams of emancipation accompanied by a reexamination of our relation to the Land of Israel. Jews fought for the rights of citizenship. Scholars emphasized the universalism of Judaism and the "mission of Israel," so they gave the Diaspora an active and more positive role than they had in the past. They minimized or rejected ties to the Land, in which very few Jews actually lived. They rarely expressed this in a *halakhic* form,[28] but usually in theological or polemic writings and most clearly in liturgical changes. One finds almost no discussion of major issues surrounding Israel in Reform responsa except those published in the last decades in Israel. Some Reform leaders changed their attitude toward Israel within a decade of the Pittsburgh Platform and were among the earliest religious Zionists. The entire movement took a positive stand toward Zionism from 1935 onward. After the establishment of Israel, the headquarters of the

World Union of Progressive Judaism moved to Israel. Reform Judaism remains Diaspora centered, however, as do Conservative Judaism and major portions of Orthodox Judaism. Those who belong to these three groups remain in the Diaspora and intend to continue their lives there.

Reform Judaism put into words what had been practiced by Jews for a long time. The Reform movement gave a religious voice to what the Jewish people had done and were continuing to do: to love Israel, but, for the vast majority, not as a home.

Secular Zionism from its earliest days has tied itself to the Bible and its ancient promises but never dealt with the *halakhic* implications that were of no interest to it. For this reason there was much rabbinic opposition to early Zionism; the Orthodox community felt that the Messianic era could not be forced. Support for Zionism came only slowly from these circles as the responsa and other literature indicated, and some opposition continues to this day.[29] The very fact that it was possible for an early Zionist Congress to debate whether resettlement should take place in the Land of Israel or in Kenya indicated the fragility of the tie to the Land. The desire for a land, a place of refuge and self-government, was almost stronger than bonds to the ancient Land of Israel. Ultimately, of course, the decision was for Israel.

CONCLUSION

The Jewish communities of the Diaspora and of Israel are now contending for primacy. Every Israeli political figure has made the demand for *aliyah,* which continues to be resisted by most Diaspora communities. Parallel to these nationalistic and political demands are religious voices that echo Nahmanides. For them the *mitzvah* of settling in the Land is primary; they feel that the divine commandments can be carried out properly only in the Land of Israel. Orthodox Jews who have resettled in Israel express these sentiments through their commitment. A smaller number of Reform Jews have also made *aliyah* for religious reasons. We now face a situation somewhat akin to that of the Hellenistic world in the first century of our era. A vigorous group within the Land of Israel claims that Jewish life can be lived there only on its terms and that nothing in the Diaspora really matters. Equally strong forces in the Diaspora contest those claims on *halakhic,* ideological, and practical grounds. More than two thousand years have shown through the choices people have made that the Diaspora is more important than the Land of Israel. Until this century love for the Land, a desire to make a pilgrimage, and the hope that an ideal state will be created there did not translate into resettlement. Most Jews continue to live outside the Land of Israel, and large numbers of Israelis regularly emigrate to the West to settle permanently. We may therefore say that the struggle for primacy will continue. The *halakhah* provides ample basis for both sides in this debate. For us in the Diaspora, however, it remains primary.

Notes

1. Jer. 42 and 44; Josephus; Philo; Maccabees 3.

2. S. Safrai and M. Stern, *The Jewish People in the First Century* (Philadelphia: Jewish Publication Society, 1974), Vol. 1, pp. 117 ff; G.Vermès, F. Millar, M. Goodman (eds.); E. Schürer, *The History of the Jewish People in the Age of Jesus Christ* (Edinburgh: 1986), Vol. 3, Part 1, pp. 3ff.

3. New Testament: Letter to the Romans, Corinthians, Galatians, et al.

THE PRIMACY OF THE DIASPORA

4. Salo W. Baron, *A Social and Religious History of the Jews* (New York: 1952), Vol. 1, pp. 172ff; Salo W. Baron, "Reflections on Ancient and Medieval Jewish Historical Demography," *Ancient and Medieval Jewish History* (New Brunswick: Rutgers University Press, 1972), pp. 10ff.

5. *Ket* 111a; *J. Sotah* 8.4.

6. *M. Kid* 1.9; *Ter* 1.5; *Sheb.* 6.6; *Hul* 410; etc.

7. *M. Orlah* 3.9; *Ter* 2.13; *Shev* 6.1; *Dem* 1.3 etc.

8. *Kid* 77a; *Men* 68b; *B.B.* 56a; B.M. 89a; *Hag* 3b; *Meg* 10a, f; *Yeb* 82b; *J. Shev* 6.1, etc.

9. *Tanhuma, Re'eh* 8; *Tanhuma, Bambidbar* 17; J. *Shev* 6.1; *Yad Hil.Ter* 1.5; *Bet Hebehirah* 6.16; etc.

10. Yehudah Halevi, Maimonides, Gersonides, Azulai, Nahmanides.

11. *Ket* 111a; Song of Songs *Rabba* 2.7; *Mekhilta* Ex 13.17; etc.

12. Moshe Gil, *A History of Palestine* (634-1099) (Cambridge: 1992), p. 67, note 70.

13. M. Avi-Yonah, *The Jews of Palestine* (New York: 1976), pp. 150ff; Gedaliah Alon, *The Jews in Their Land in the Talmudic Age* (Jerusalem: 1980), Vol. 2.

14. Gil, op. cit., pp. 624ff.

15. Gil, op. cit., 633.

16. Gil, op. cit., 612ff.

17. Hai Gaon in *Otzar Hageonim Ketuvot* 836; Isaac Schepansky, *Eretz Yisrael Besafrut Hateshuvot* (Jerusalem 1966) Vol. 1, pp. 119ff. These citations take us into the fourteenth century.

18. *Teshuvot Rambam* (ed. Blau) (Jerusalem: 1958), (2), 639ff.

19. S. D. Goitein, *A Mediterranean Society* (Berkeley: University of California Press, 1971), Vol. 2, p. 12ff.

20. Ephraim Karnafogel, "*Aliyah* of Three Hundred Rabbis," *Jewish Quarterly Review* 76 (1985), pp. 193f.

21. Schepansky, op. cit., Vol. 1, pp. 120f.

22. Schepansky, op. cit., Vol. 1, pp. 133f.

23. Efraim Urbach, *Ba-alei Tosfot* (Jerusalem, 1955), pp. 320f.

24. Comment to Moses Maimonides, *Sefer Mitzvot*, Aseh 4.

25. Abraham b. Isaac of Narbonne (1110–1179), *Sefer Ha-eshkol;* Isaac ben Abba Mari (1122–1193), *Itur;* Asher ben Yehiel (1250–1328), *Halakhot;* Isaac ben Moses of Vienna (1200–1270), *Or Zarua;* Moses ben Jacob of Coucy (thirteenth century), *Sefer Hamitzvot;* Isaac ben Joseph of Corbeil (thirteenth century), *Kol Bo;* Jacob ben Asher (died 1340), *Baal Haturim;* etc.

26. Israel Schepansky, *Eretz Yisrael Besafrut Hateshuvot* (Jerusalem, 1966). This three-volume work contains all the relevant material; as one-third of it is from the last two centuries, we can see the limited inquiries made in the preceding thousand years.

27. Moshe Idel, "The Land of Israel in Medieval Kabbalah," in Lawrence A. Hoffman (ed.), *The Land of Israel, Jewish Perspectives* (South Bend: Notre Dame University Press, 1986), pp. 170ff.

28. W. Jacob (ed.), *The Changing World of Reform Judaism—The Pittsburgh Platform in Retrospect* (Pittsburgh 1985), pp. 25ff., pp. 108ff.

29. Israel Schepansky, op. cit., Vol. 3.

SELECTED REFORM RESPONSA

These responsa on are a representative selection from more than one thousand American Reform responsa published in the twentieth century. We are grateful to the Central Conference of American Rabbis and the Hebrew Union College Press for permission to reproduce them.

ISRAELI FLAG ON A SYNAGOGUE PULPIT

Walter Jacob

QUESTION: Should an Israeli flag be displayed on the pulpit of an American Reform Synagogue? In this case an American flag is already so displayed (Rabbi R. Goldman, Chattanooga, Tennessee)*

ANSWER: The six-pointed Star of David is now commonly recognized as a symbol of Jews and Judaism throughout the world, both by ourselves and by our non-Jewish neighbors. There is no clear distinction between Jews and Judaism, between our religious and our national aspirations. Since the Babylonian Diaspora, our prayers have constantly contained petitions for the return to Zion and the reestablishment of Israel. In the traditional Shabbat morning Torah service we find an additional prayer (a) for the academies in Israel, Babylonia, and the Diaspora; (b) for the local congregation; and (c) for the Gentile government under which we live *(Abudarham, 47b; Machzor Vitry; Rokeach)*. These prayers have been part of the service either since the Talmudic period or, at the latest, since the fourteenth century. In other words, the service has for a long time contained side-by-side prayers expressing the desire for a return to the Land of Israel, gratitude for the land in which we live, and hope for the welfare of our own communities. The flags of the United States and Israel on a pulpit might be said to symbolize the prayers that have always been said in the synagogue. For this reason there is no religious objection to placing an American flag on the pulpit nor in placing an Israeli flag alongside it. (Of course, there are secular regulations for placing such flags, and these should be followed.) It might be helpful to look at the historical background, especially as there is no ancient record of a Jewish flag or symbol for the entire people of Israel.

The six-pointed star was rarely used by the early Jewish community. It is found carved on a stone in the Capernaum synagogue and also on a single tombstone in Tarentum, Italy, that dates from the third century. Later Kabbalists used it, probably borrowing it from the Templars (Ludwig Blau, "Magen David," *Jewish Encyclopedia,* Vol. 8, p. 252). It is also found in some non-Kabbalistic medieval manuscripts. None of these usages, however, was widespread.

A Jewish flag is mentioned for the first time during the rule of Charles IV of Hungary, who prescribed in 1354 that the Jews of Prague use a red flag with David's and Solomon's seal. Also, in the fifteenth century, the Jews of that city met King Matthias with a red flag featuring two golden six-pointed stars and two five-pointed stars. Aside from this, we have no record of any Jewish community using a flag, and, of course, the six-pointed star now so commonly seen was rarely used as a Jewish symbol before the late eighteenth and early nineteenth centuries. Then, the newly emancipated Jewish community wanted an easily recognizable symbol akin to that of Christianity and so adopted the six-pointed star, which was then used frequently on books, synagogues, cemeteries, tombstones, and so on. The star soon became recognized as a sign of Judaism: by 1799 it was already used in anti-Semitic literature. In 1822 the Rothschilds used it for their coat of arms, and in 1897 the Zionist Congress in Basel adopted it as its symbol. Subsequently, the State of Israel used it in its national flag, although the official symbol of Israel is the Menorah. Naturally, all of us also remember the times when we were forced to use the six-pointed star on badges that identified us to hostile neighbors.

If you wish detailed information on this material see M. Gruenwald, "Ein Altes Symbol," *Jahrbuch fuer juedische Literatur,* 1901, pp. 120ff; L. Blau, "Magen David," *Jewish Encyclopedia,* Vol. 8, pp. 25f; and G. Scholem, "Mogen David," *Encyclopedia Judaica,* Vol. 11, pp. 687ff.

Various synagogues have found other solutions to the desire to honor both the United States and Israel. Thus, some have placed both flags in the foyer off the community hall but have no flags on the pulpits. In any case, both the loyalty of our communities to the United States and our common concern for Israel are clear with or without the placement or possession of flags.

---

*Walter Jacob, *American Reform Responsa* (New York: Central Conference of American Rabbis, 1983), No. 22.

AN OLD ISRAELI FLAG

Walter Jacob

QUESTION: An Israeli flag which has stood on our pulpit for some time is now worn out. How should we dispose of it? (Morton Kramer, Los Angeles, California)*

ANSWER: Special honors have been accorded to the various appurtenances of the synagogue that possess different degrees of sacredness. Sacred texts and the Torah were buried or set aside in a safe place (Rashi to *Ket.* 19b; *Shulhan Arukh* Orah Hayim 154.5). They were sometimes interred with a scholar. Items that were a little more distant, like the cover of a Torah and a binder, were also sometimes buried with a scholar. Still other synagogue decorations, as for example, the cover of the bimah, could be renewed and the old item discarded.

Although the Israeli flag may stand on the bimah, it possesses no degree of sacredness. It is a symbol of the State of Israel but has no specific religious connotation, so we need take no unusual care for religious reasons. There are, of course, other reasons for disposing of a flag appropriately. We do so with the American flag in accordance with specific regulations and would accord similar respect to the flag of Israel. The attitude toward flags has changed in various periods, as we have seen from recent discussions about the burning of the American flag as well as its use on shirts, jackets, and the like.

SELECTED REFORM RESPONSA

No degree of sacredness is connected with the Israeli flag despite its place on the pulpit. We should dispose of a worn flag in a dignified way, but not as a sacred object.

*Walter Jacob, "Questions and Reform Jewish Answers," *New American Reform Responsa* (Central Conference of American Rabbis, New York, 1992).

HEBREW OR ENGLISH AT AN ISRAELI SERVICE

Walter Jacob

QUESTION: My family and I spend a part of each year in Israel. Although we are beginning to feel at home with spoken Hebrew, it remains rather basic, and we feel ill at ease in the Liberal Jewish services which we have attended. We would like to establish a service which will use English. That effort has been discouraged by various individuals who felt that this was inappropriate in Israel and that it would hurt the Liberal movement in Israel. May we use a service which contains a considerable amount of English in Israel? (Norman Miller, Tel Aviv, Israel)*

ANSWER: Problems with the lack of familiarity with Hebrew are very ancient. Ezra had to explain the Torah to the exiles who returned from Babylon (Neh. 8:7). The Torah and other sections of the Bible were subsequently translated into Aramaic as well as Greek so they could be properly understood.

We find some discussion of the language to be used in prayers both in the Mishnah and the Talmud. Permission to recite basic prayers in the vernacular was granted quite early (M Sotah 7.1; 32bff). Such decisions in favor of the vernacular were carried into all the great codifications of Jewish law (*Yad Hil Qeriat Shema* 2.10; *Tur* and *Shulhan Arukh* Orah Hayim 62;101). In addition to this, of course, many devotional volumes and books of women's prayers were written in the vernacular throughout the Middle Ages (Solomon B. Freehof, "Devotional Literature in the Vernacular," *Central Conference of American Rabbis Yearbook,* Vol. 33, pp. 380ff). Reform prayer books began to use the vernacular in Europe and in the United States. The earliest such liturgy is the Charleston, South Carolina, prayer book of 1824. We have continued to use the vernacular alongside Hebrew in lands throughout the world. The amount of Hebrew in our services has varied from one locale to another, but we have always retained enough Hebrew to continue a strong bond with the tradition, and enough vernacular to enable our congregants to understand the prayers and to recite them with appropriate devotion and not by rote. This should also be the goal of your services in Israel.

During this period when English remains your primary tongue and the local Liberal services are therefore not meaningful, there is nothing wrong with starting another service for your family and friends that follows the American *minhag* and contains some English. We should remember that *minhagim* connected with ritual, poetry, melodies, and language were often continued by immigrants or long-term visitors in the land in which they found themselves. Since the first century, synagogues in Israel were identified as Babylonian, which meant that they followed Babylonian rites and possibly some Aramaic. Later, of course, many Aramaic prayers were added to all services. In the Middle Ages the immigration of *Sephardim* to *Ashkenazi* lands led to debates and acrimony as local congregations sought to impose a single *minhag* on all Jews in their locale (David Cohen of Corfu, Responsa 11; Moses of Trani, Responsa Vol. 1, No. 307; etc). Such efforts to establish uniformity inevitably failed. In the United States each group that arrived brought its own *minhagim,* and these included variations in liturgy and melody. There would be nothing improper about establishing a minyan that had a service partially in English for the benefit of your friends and family.

*Walter Jacob, "Questions and Reform Jewish Answers," *New American Reform Responsa* (New York: Conference of American Rabbis, 1992).

POPULAR ISRAELI SONG IN THE SYNAGOGUE

Walter Jacob

QUESTION: A youngster in our community has brought an Israeli melody back from a visit to Israel. The words which usually accompany it are rather wild, but he has successfully set a portion of our liturgy to it and it has become popular with our young people. Should this adaption be permitted? (Lloyd Lehman, Los Angeles, California)*

ANSWER: The sources of Jewish music are varied. Some of our music can be traced to melodies used in the ancient Temple (E. Werner, "The Sacred Bridge: A Voice Still Heard"; A. Z. Idelsohn, "Jewish Music"). Other melodies were soon forgotten by the general public but continued in Jewish liturgical use.

There would be problems using the melody you have described in an Israeli setting. There, the association with the profane words would make it objectionable to those acquainted with the song. In our American setting the words are not known, so we are simply left with an appealing melody. The song will probably be quickly forgotten in Israel and its place taken by other pop tunes. It may, however, survive its American liturgical setting and so add to our musical heritage.

---

*Walter Jacob, "Questions and Reform Jewish Answers" *New American Reform Responsa* (New York: Central Conference of American Rabbis, 1992), No. 18.

JERUSALEM SOIL INTO THE GRAVE

Walter Jacob

QUESTION: A relative of the deceased has brought some soil from Jerusalem which he wishes the family to place in the coffin. The burial took place some months earlier; should the grave be opened in order to do this? What is the origin of the custom of burying with a vial of such soil? (Hannah Smith, Seattle, Washington)[*]

ANSWER: Burial in the Land of Israel has been sought by the pious through the ages. Jacob the Patriarch and, later, his son Joseph were taken from Egypt to be buried in Israel (Gen 49:31; 50:13). When this was impossible, some pious individuals traveled to Israel in their old age so that they might die and be buried there. As according to some speculations, resurrection of the dead will begin with the Land of Israel, burial there would ensure earlier resurrection.

In our century burials may be arranged in Israel, and some Orthodox families have done so. Others have sought to emphasize their ties with Israel by including a vial of soil from Jerusalem in their coffin. I have found no traditional sources that mention this custom.

A body may be exhumed for a variety of reasons, including reburial in Israel (*Shulhan Arukh* Yoreh Deah 363.1ff), but not to place a vial of Israeli soil in the coffin. It would be appropriate to sprinkle that soil onto the existing grave without disturbing it, thereby satisfying the wishes of the visiting relative.

*Walter Jacob,"Questions and Reform Jewish Answers" (New American Responsa (New York: Central Conference of American Rabbis, 1992), No.174.

VISITING ISRAEL

Solomon B. Freehof

QUESTION: A couple saved for years to visit Israel for a month. But now they plan to use the money for the college expenses of their children. Have they the right to do so? Is it not a supreme, religious duty to go to Palestine? (Rabbi Allen S. Maller, Culver City, California)*

ANSWER: A person nowadays may want to go to the Land of Israel and consider his visit to be a moral obligation. In that case it is a matter for him to decide how important this is to him in comparison with other uses for his money. But the question here is a deeper one than a sense of group commitment or pride. It is a question of religious duty. Is it a religious duty to go to Palestine and does one violate any religious duty if one fails to do so?

This question of whether it is a religious obligation to settle in the Holy Land has been discussed since the Middle Ages and, interestingly enough, has become again from the *halakhic* point of view the subject of a rather heated discussion in our day. The Chassidim, especially the Satmar group, who consider themselves the most completely and uncompromisingly religious of all Jews, are also bitterly opposed to the modern State of Israel. It is therefore necessary for them (and for those who are like-minded) to come to terms with this religious question. Because of this deep concern on the part of these anti-modern-Israel Orthodox Jews, a considerable literature has grown up on this subject. The most important is the collection by Moses Bloch in three volumes of a work called *Dovev Sifse Yeshenim,* in which he gathers all the opinions of the Orthodox rabbinate of the last hundred years against a modern Jewish state and the plans to establish it. The very first letter in the first volume is typical and representative. It is by the famous scholar Jacob of Lissa, addressed to the pioneer protagonist of religious Zionism, Rabbi Zvi Hirsch Kalisch. Virtually all the Orthodox arguments on the anti-Zionist side of the question are marshaled here (as they are in the subsequent letters). It is important in our attempt to solve this question of religious obligation to go through the law systematically. The basis of the law is the very last Mishnah in the tractate *Ketubah* which we are told that a husband may compel his wife to emigrate with him to the Holy Land. If she refuses he can divorce her without even giving her the money stipulated in her *ketubah*. Rashi (in the Talmud, *Ketubah* 110b) says this means a man may compel not only his wife, but his entire family to settle in the Holy Land.

The Tosfos to this passage, however, says that this law does not apply today because it is dangerous to travel there (this was the eleventh century). The Tosfos further quotes Rabbi Haim, who gives a second reason why it is no longer a religious duty to settle there: namely, that there are many important commandments that apply to the Holy Land and that a man may be unable to fulfill nowadays.

This negative point of view is contravened by many other authorities. Nahmanides counts settlement in the Holy Land as one of the *mitzvot*. Isserlein (fourteenth century) in his *Pesakim* 88, acknowledges the great dangers of settlement but says that a man should judge whether he can endure and fulfill the commandments; if he can, he should settle there. The Mordecai (Mordecai ben Hillel, fourteenth century) quotes the Tosfos on the danger of travel and settlement and says that the law therefore is that a husband may not compel a wife to go with him there. Caro (*Shulhan Arukh,* Even

Hoezer 75, 4 and 5) first states the law definitely that a husband may compel a wife to settle in the Holy Land with him but adds, then, "Some say it is dangerous and a man has no right to bring himself or others into danger; therefore (if the journey is short) from Alexandria eastward, he may compel his wife to go with him; but if they live west of Alexandria he may not." Hayim Benvenisti (Turkey, seventeenth century) in his *Keneses Hagdola* to Bes Joseph, Even Hoezer 75, marshals all the arguments on both sides and tends to agree with the above compromise opinion Caro takes in the *Shulhan Arukh*.

There is an interesting discussion of the question from Prague at the end of the seventeenth and the beginning of the eighteenth century. It is a responsum by Jonah Landsofer in his *M'il S'daka* 26. The circumstances are interesting enough to deserve mention. A group of three men decided to settle in the Land and take with them their young children, aged three and four. Many people raised the objection that they had no right to endanger the little children on this perilous journey. Landsofer answers that the commandment to settle in the Land is eternal. As for the dangers that may vary from time to time and place, they must, of course, be considered when we discuss the question of whether a man may compel his family to go with him. But aside from the question of the rights of his wife, if there is not too much danger, it is just as safe for the children as for the adults. A fair statement of the law is to be found in the balanced opinion reached in the *Be'er Hetev* (Judah of Tiktin) to the passage. He says, "Since the question of whether it is a religious duty is a subject of disagreement among the great teachers, it is clear, then, that a man may not compel his wife to move with him to the Holy Land. See also Igros Moshe Hoezer 102 (end), where he says that it is a *mitzvah* for Palestinians to dwell in Israel but there is no mandatory *mitzvah* for others to live there.

The question of the religious duty to the Holy Land can be considered a moot question in which, therefore, compulsion of husband against wife may not be applied. For the sake of completeness, we ought to mention that there was a great deal of *halakhic* debate on the reverse of our question; namely, whether a person already settled in the Holy Land ought emigrate to live in the Diaspora. For a full discussion of this question, see *Treasury of Responsa,* pp. 167ff., where there is an account of the responsum on this subject by Yom Tov Zahalon (1557-1638), Rabbi of Safed.

Returning to the case discussed here, it is not even a question of settling in the Holy Land but a question merely of going there for a brief visit. In that regard there is not, as far as I know, any authoritative opinion at all to the effect that a brief visit is to be considered a religious duty.

Now, as to the children, if it were a question of the study of the Torah, let us say it was a choice between the parents' going to Israel and the children studying in the Yeshiva, that question could possibly enter into the discussion. Isserlein cites the fact that in his day there was very little Talmudic study in Israel, and that fact was used as an argument against settling there. But secular education has no standing in Jewish law (although under special circumstances it is permitted), and therefore college education, unlike Talmudic education, could not be weighed against settlement. Nowadays, of course, with the many yeshivot in Israel, according to the recent official Mizrachi magazine, there is a large Orthodox settlement from the yeshivot in America. These yeshiva heads and students are confident that they can fulfill their religious duties all the better in Israel and hence follow the caution of Israel Isserlein.

In the case mentioned, however, it is first of all not a question of settlement, but of a visit, which is no particular *mitzvah,* and secondly a question of an education that is of no concern in Jewish law. In this case, therefore, the parents may do as they wish.

*Solomon B. Freehof, *Contemporary Reform Responsa,* No.15 (Cincinnati: Hebrew Union College, 1974).

ALIYAH IN FACE OF PARENTAL OPPOSITION

Moshe Zemer

QUESTION: A young man who had just graduated from university is preparing to go on *aliyah* to Israel. His parents strenuously object. They claim that he has visited Israel many times since childhood and may go there as often as he wants in the future. If their only son leaves them he will dishonor them instead of fulfilling the commandment to "Honor your father and your mother." The son counters that his decision was influenced by the Jewish education and the love of Israel that his parents instilled in him. Is there in Jewish law a resolution to this dissension?

ANSWER: We have here a conflict in the observance of two *mitzvot*. On the one hand it has been argued that the Fifth Commandment, "Honor your father and your mother" (Exod. 20:11; Deut. 5:15) is of supreme importance. The thirteenth-century author of *Sefer Ha-hinukh* claimed:

> You should be mindful that your father and mother are the reason for your existence in the world. Therefore, it is indeed appropriate that you render to them all the honor and beneficence that you can (*Sefer Ha-hinukh,* ed. Chavell, Jerusalem, 1988, no. 28, p. 79).

On the other hand, great *halakhists* decided that *aliyah* is paramount. Maimonides (1138-1204) decided that settling in *Eretz Yisrael* is a rabbinic ordinance *(mitzvah d'rabban):* "One should always live in the Land of Israel" (*Hilkot Melakhim* 5:12). Nahmanides (Gerona, Spain, 1195-1270) ruled that settling the Land of Israel is a biblical precept and divine commandment equal to all others in the Torah (*Sefer Hamitzvot,* gloss to positive precept 4).

Since honoring one's parents and settling the Land of Israel are both *mitzvot,* does one of them take precedence? Rabbi Meir ben Baruch, the Maharam of Rothenburg (1215–1293), answered this question seven hundred years ago in the following responsum:

> You have asked if a father may prevent his son from going on *aliyah* to Israel. Since it has been established that *aliyah* to the Land of Israel is a *mitzvah,* and each such *mitzvah* is followed by "I am the Lord," which means that you should not obey your parent when he commands you to violate a *mitzvah,* because the honor due to God takes precedence (*Responsa Maharam ben Barukh,* no. 79).

The honor due one's parents is not unlimited. Parents do not have to be obeyed when they demand that their child violate a Torah commandment.

The conflict between parents and children about *aliyah* continued throughout the centuries. Rabbi Moses ben Joseph Trani, known by his acronym, Mabit, was the rabbi of Safed in the sixteenth century. He received a question about a young man who had made a vow to go on *aliyah* and settle in the Galilee. His father and mother, however, did not allow him to go. The questioner asks: "Teach us, our Rabbi, if the vow is valid and binding, or may he be released from it."

This family dissonance results from the above noted, seemingly irreconcilable conflict between two Torah commandments: filial respect and *aliyah* to the Holy Land. If the son capitulates to his parents' demand he will be prevented from observing the precept of dwelling in the Land. If, in spite of their pleading, he does emigrate, it would appear that he is not honoring his parents.

The Mabit responded that "he neither has to fulfill his vow nor is obligated to obey his father and mother, who told him not to go on *aliyah,* " just as he is not obliged to observe their command to violate any other commandment. The Mabit uses the same argument as the Maharam of Rothenburg that the honor due to God and the *mitzvot* of the Torah must be preferred over filial respect. The Rabbi of Safed finally resolves this conflict with a creative *halakhic* verdict:

> Both son and father are commanded to dwell in the Land of Israel. The son is not liable for not observing the *mitzvah* of honoring his parents (by remaining in the Diaspora), because they can also go on *aliyah* with him and thereby both the commandments of dwelling in the Land and filial respect will be fulfilled (*Responsa Mabit* 1, no. 139).

Although this radical solution would not seem appropriate to the question before us, it does reflect a major line of *halakhic* reasoning. It would appear that the parents of the young man in our case have an unexpressed agenda. They are fearful that their son will be lost to them. The reality is that many daughters and sons who live abroad are closer to their parents than are others who live in the same city. With modern transportation and communications they can maintain close contact. It is not the physical closeness alone that determines the quality of a relationship, but rather the love, understanding, and consideration for one another. Parents raise their children to make mature life decisions, including their choice of profession and mate. Thus, the parents of this young man may be justly proud that their son has made a courageous decision about his future home.

The parents assert that visiting Israel should be enough for their son. This young man apparently prefers the stance of Rabbi Joseph Trani (son of the Mabit), who stated that "the essence of the *mitzvah* is not *aliyah,* but dwelling in the Land and establishing a home there, as the late Nahmanides taught. Anyone who goes there as a tourist intending to return whence he came is not fulfilling the well-known *mitzvah"* *(Responsa Maharit,* 2, no. 28).

Furthermore, if his father and mother supported their son's decision, he would most likely fulfill the teaching of Rabbi Simeon ben Zemah Duran (Rashbatz, 1361-1444), who ruled that going abroad from the Land of Israel is permitted for only two purposes, one of which is to visit his mother and father to fulfill the honor due one's parents *(Responsa Tashbetz,* 3, no. 288). The son or daughter is duty bound to maintain contact with father and mother, including traveling from the Land to the parents' home. If this was the case in the fourteenth and fifteenth centuries, when journeying abroad was dangerous and took many months, how much more is it a *mitzvah* in our day. Although the physical distance may be great, parents and children may be drawn closer together.

QUESTIONS FROM ISRAEL ON PROSELYTISM

Solomon B. Freehof

QUESTION: How does American Reform Judaism view conversion, what is required in contrast to the tradition? Let me also ask a series of brief other questions on matters connected with conversion. (D. Moaz, Jerusalem)*

ANSWER: I shall be glad to answer your letter of July 29, but it is not possible to give a simple and direct answer to each of your questions in the order you presented them. The reason this is difficult is that some of the questions require an explanation of the basic philosophy of the Reform movement, and it would be misleading simply to say "yes" or "no." This situation applies especially to Question 1, to what extent does proselytism by a Reform rabbi meet the requirements of the *halakha* as to (a) circumcision *(brith-mila);* (b) baptism *(tevila);* (c) acceptance of the commandments *(kabalat ol mitzvot).* If I answered simply that we do not do (a) or (b) or (c), I would fail to explain the reason for our basic attitude in such matters.

The attitude of Reform Judaism on ceremonial commandments is that they are secondary to the moral and doctrinal commandments. So our emphasis in proselytism is as follows: We do not *require* as an absolute prerequisite either circumcision or *tevila* but lay great emphasis on the instructions. This should not surprise you, for it is possible according to the *halakhah* to conceive of a conversion without circumcision or the *mikvah* because this was the very subject of the debate in the Talmud *(Yevamoth 46a)* where some of the authorities believe that a proselyte is a full proselyte even without circumcision or *mikvah*.

But the debate in the Talmud is not the real reason for our practice. Our general philosophy is that the ethical and philosophical meaning of Judaism is more the essential than the ceremonial. We may correctly say, therefore, that less emphasis is placed on circumcision and *mikvah* and more on instruction. That is to say, it is not the mood of Reform to *abolish* the first two rituals. Some rabbis require it, some do not. In some countries the Reform movement requires it and in some countries it does not. In ceremonial matters we avoid strictness; but on the third element, namely, instruction, we put our great emphasis. In this regard, if I may say so, our method of accepting proselytes is superior to that of Orthodoxy. In Orthodoxy instruction is comparatively minor, although it is indeed required. With us it is major. Most large congregations have a class of proselytes whose instruction will last a half or even a whole year; and as you may well imagine, whereas we teach the various home ceremonies that the candidate will observe (such as Friday night lighting of the candles, etc), our main emphasis in this long instruction is on Jewish history, Jewish writings, Jewish ethics. Forgive this long answer. A short answer would have been no answer at all.

Now with regard to other questions, some I will answer simply "yes" or "no," but with others I will give you a specific case that shows you how it was answered.

2. Proselytism for material purposes, etc: We examine the candidates carefully to make sure that they have serious and worthy

motives leading them to the desire to become Jewish. The difference between us and Orthodoxy, however, is this: Theoretically, but not actually, in Orthodoxy if a person comes to be converted for the purpose of marrying a Jew, this is deemed unworthy, but with us, we consider that the desire to establish a home of unified spiritual mood is a worthy motive. We do not consider that if a candidate wants to be married to a Jew this is unworthy at all. See the relevant section from the report of the Central Conference of American Rabbis on "Mixed Marriages and Intermarriage," *CCAR Yearbook 57,* 1947. This also answers Question 3.

4. Attitude toward a proselyte and a Cohen: Reform Judaism has abolished all differences in religious standing between Cohanim, Leviim, and other Jews. We are all deemed equal. Question 4, therefore, has no meaning for us.

5. A proselyte continuing with his non-Jewish spouse: We would consider this wrong for the reason indicated in a responsum that I wrote a few years ago that was published in the CCAR *Journal* and is found in *Current Reform Responsa,* p. 215.

6. Could a minor proselyte without his parents? No, we would not break up a family. With the consent of his parents, certainly. This is already mentioned in the Talmud in *Ketubah* 11a.

7. As to the status of a minor who did not proselytize while his parents did, we have made a new provision for children whose parents have become Jewish. The change is in accordance with our general principle: Since the ceremonials of circumcision and *mikvah* are not so important to us as the instruction, we have decided that if such parents wish their child to be Jewish and enter him in our

school, when he graduates (or is confirmed, usually around the age of fourteen) this is deemed with us to be full and official conversion of the child.

8. To answer this question I must first answer 13e: Is there supreme *halakhic* authority in Reform Judaism? No, the Central Conference of American Rabbis and our other organizations, such as the Union of American Hebrew Congregations, are voluntary organizations for consultation and mutual guidance. We have at the Conference a Responsa Committee of which I have the honor to be chairman. My decisions in answer to questions are made according to what seems to me a balance between the attitude of the *halakha* and the needs of modern times. The decisions are meant for guidance and not for governance. We respect the *halakha* as an expression of Jewish spiritual thought and feeling for two thousand years, and we follow it whenever we deem it possible to do so.

Now, therefore the question of No. 8: The Conference is opposed to the marriage of a Jew with an unconverted non-Jew. A few rabbis, nevertheless, do officiate at such marriages. They are a small minority. Even these few do not officiate indiscriminately, but only under special circumstances as, for example, if the couple are both old people or if they had been married already in the civil courts and the husband is going overseas to serve in the Armed Forces, and so on. So your question deals only with a few special cases, and we have not yet come to a conclusion as to what the status of such children should be.

9. Should the laws of proselytism be changed according to the principle of *Hora'at Sha'ah?* We think so. That is really the

mood of Reform Judaism, but the motive for change must be a serious one.

10. Could a non-Jew become a Jew other than by proselytization? No.

11. Differences in Israel and abroad: my *personal* judgment is that proselytization should be made easier in Israel because the whole environment is Jewish and it is almost inevitable that a home in which one member is a convert will be a truly Jewish home.

12. Is Judaism a nationality or a religion or both? The question would make more sense in eastern Europe than in the western democratic countries. In eastern Europe as, for example, in Soviet Russia, historic groups are considered separate nationalities. In western democratic nations each person is an individual. A nation comprises individuals of equal status, with no separate grouping of nationalities.

Nevertheless, our sense of historic unity and our brotherly bond with the State of Israel is deep and real. The best description of Judaism according to the feeling of most Reform Jews is that we are a religion and a family, with all the intimate relationships that the word "family" implies. This is in accordance with the spirit of Jewish law. A convert is converted not merely to a religion, but to a real kinship. He or she may now marry a Jew and is always part of the Jewish family. In fact, the historic phrase that a convert is like a newborn child is an exact expression of somebody being reborn (*Yevamoth* 22a).

13a, b, b-1: In actual practice only a rabbi officiates, but according to Jewish law, if necessary a non-rabbi can conduct a conversion.

13c. The authority of *Semicha* of a Reform rabbi: Orthodox rabbis have no legal authority either. The true *Semicha* ended in the third century. What is called *Semicha* today in Orthodox life is really *Hatarat Hora'ah,* the right to teach. In other words, it is exactly equal in status to a graduation diploma. The Reform rabbi has the same rights as an Orthodox rabbi, the right conferred upon him by his education and his acceptance by a congregation. No rabbi in the world has any greater authority.

This should answer 13d, since there is no actual legal authority anywhere in the rabbinate—Orthodox, Conservative, or Reform. I would answer "yes" to d, but an Orthodox rabbi does not recognize the status of any other type of rabbi. 13e is already answered.

14. The relation of a proselyte to his former neighborhood and family: technically speaking, they do not exist for him, but as the Talmud says, he would then justly complain that has left a nobler sanctity for a lower one (*Yevamoth* 22a). Hence, in many ways traditional law recognizes the relationship that remains between the proselyte and his family. The problem arises practically in questions of whether proselytes should say *Kaddish* for their Gentile fathers. This has been answered affirmatively in Jewish law.

15a. I do not know of this occurring often, but it did occur at least once. A proselyte attains an indelible allegiance to Judaism and can never throw it off again. I know of no statistics regarding 15b or c.

16. My own experience has been that often proselyte women, especially, become more earnestly Jewish than many of their Jewish-born friends.

17. Is conversion *reshut* or *mitzvah?* This is an open question in Jewish law, and as far as the Reform movement is concerned, we still debate it among ourselves. The Union of American Hebrew Congregation, for example, passed a resolution a few years ago that we should go out and seek converts. In other words, it is a *mitzvah.* The Central Conference of American Rabbis has not yet passed on this matter. As I say, it is an open question.

---

*Solomon B. Freehof, *Contemporary Reform Responsa* (Cincinnati: Hebrew Union College, 1974), No. 1.

CONTRIBUTORS

Solomon B. Freehof - (1893-1990) Rabbi of the Rodef Shalom Congregation, Pittsburgh, Pennsylvania; President of the Central Conference of American Rabbis, and the World Union for Progressive Judaism; Chair of the Responsa Committee of the Central Conference of American Rabbis. Author of eight volumes of responsa including *Today's Reform Responsa* (1990), as well as *Reform Jewish Practice* (1947, 1952), *The Responsa Literature* (1955), *A Treasury of Responsa* (1963) and many other books.

Judith Hauptman - Associate Professor of Talmud, Jewish Theological Seminary; formerly Visiting Assistant Professor of Talmud, Hebrew Union College, New York. Author of "Images and Women in the Talmud" and *The Development of the Talmudic Sugya*.

Leonard Kravitz - Professor of Midrash and Homiletics at the Hebrew Union College - Jewish Institute of Religion in New York. He has served on the Medical Ethics Committee of the New York Federation of Philanthropies. Author of *The Esoteric Meaning of Maimonides' Guide for the Perplexed* (1988), *Commentary on the Ethics of the Fathers* (1992) with K. Olitzky.

Walter Jacob - Senior Scholar of Rodef Shalom Congregation, Pittsburgh, Pennsylvania; Past President of the Central Conference of American Rabbis, Chair of the Responsa Committee; President of the Freehof Institute of Progressive *Halakhah*. Author and editor of twenty books including *American Reform Responsa* (1983), *Contemporary American Reform Responsa* (1987), *Liberal Judaism and Halakhah* (1988), *Questions and Reform Jewish-Answers - New Reform Responsa* (1991), *The Healing Past: Pharmaceuticals in the Biblical and Rabbinic World* (1993).

John D. Rayner - A graduate of Cambridge University and the Hebrew Union College. Rabbi Emeritus of the Liberal Jewish Synagogue, London, England and Lecturer in Liturgy and Codes at the Leo Baeck College.

Aviezer Ravitzky - Professor of Jewish Philosophy and Chairman of the Department of Jewish Studies at the Hebrew University, Jerusalem. Visiting Professor at Rice, Harvard, Pennsylvania, Yeshiva, and Brown Universities. Author of numerous books, including *Messianism, Zionism and Jewish Religious Radicalism* (1996).

Moshe Zemer - Director of the Freehof Institute of Progressive *Halakhah*; a founder of the Movement for Progressive Judaism in Israel; founding rabbi of the Kedem Synagogue-Bet Daniel, Tel Aviv. *Av Bet Din* of the Israel Council of Progressive Rabbis, Senior Lecturer in Rabbinic at the Hebrew Union College, Jerusalem. Contributor of numerous articles on *halakhah* in the Israeli press and scientific journals; author of *The Sane Halakhah* [Hebrew], (1993).

www.ingramcontent.com/pod-product-compliance
Lightning Source LLC
Chambersburg PA
CBHW052020290426
44112CB00014B/2318